John Pinkerton, Sir David Lindsay

Scotish Poems

Vol. 3

John Pinkerton, Sir David Lindsay

Scotish Poems
Vol. 3

ISBN/EAN: 9783744715560

Printed in Europe, USA, Canada, Australia, Japan

Cover: Foto ©Thomas Meinert / pixelio.de

More available books at **www.hansebooks.com**

SCOTISH POEMS,

REPRINTED

FROM SCARCE EDITIONS.

THE TALES OF THE PRIESTS OF PEBLIS.	PHILOTUS, A COMEDY.
THE PALICE OF HONOUR.	GAWAN AND GOLOGRAS, A METRICAL ROMANCE.
SQUIRE MELDRUM.	BALLADS, FIRST PRINTED
EIGHT INTERLUDES, BY DAVID LINDSAY.	AT EDINBURGH, 1508.

WITH THREE PIECES BEFORE UNPUBLISHED.

———————————

COLLECTED BY JOHN PINKERTON,

F.S.A. PERTH, HONORARY MEMBER OF THE ROYAL SOCIETY OF ICELANDIC LITERATURE AT COPENHAGEN, AND OF THE ROYAL SOCIETY OF SCIENCES AT DRONTHEIM.

IN THREE VOLUMES.

———————————

VOLUME III.

———————————

LONDON:

PRINTED BY AND FOR JOHN NICHOLS.

M,DCC,XCII.

C O N T E N T S

OF

V O L U M E III.

ERRATA in VOLUME III.

Page 86, line 16, *for* never *read* ever.

99, 13, *for* n *read* in.

102, *put a space—at the word* fprang, ft. xv, *as a new Adventure there begins.*

114, line *pen. for* ane *read* pane.

136, 13, *for* 1503 *read* 1504.

151, 22, *for* uay *read* nay.

161, 14, *for* their *read* cleir.

163, 15, *for* fome *read* fone.

—— 17, *for* in vairt *read* invairt.

165, 5, *for* lere *read* tere.

169, 14, 16, 18, 20, *read* levit, brevit, chevit, levit.

172, 12, *for* all yace *read* allyace.

—— 15, *put a* comma *inftead of the* full-point.

—— 16, *put a* full-point *inftead of the* comma.

—— — *firft note,* delete *MS. margin, for* it is a note of the Editor; and place thefe words after the *fecond note,*

187, 12, *for* ll *read* All.

192, 17, *for* Kingis *read* King is.

201, after line 4, a line is wanting.

211, line 16, *for* Arthur gives Galaron *read* gives Gawan.

Ane verie excellent and delecta-
bill Treatife*, intitulit

P H I L O T U S,

Quhairin we may perfave the .
greit Inconveniences that fallis out in the
Mariage betwene Age and Youth.

OVID.
Siqua velis aptè nubere, nube pari.

Imprinted at EDINBURGH
be ROBERT CHARTERIS, 1603.
Cum Privilegio Regis.

* Comedie. Edit. Edinb. 1612, 4to.

THE NAMES OF THE INTERLOQUITORS.

THE ARGUMENT.

(From the Edition of 1612, Edinb. 4to.)

PHILOTUS, an olde rich man, is enamoured with the love of EMILIA, daughter to ALBERTO, who being refufed, imployeth a MACRELL, or pandrous, to al- lure her thereto, but all in vain; afterward he dealeth with her father ALBERTO, who being blinded with the man's wealth, ufeth firft faire words, and thereafter threatnings, to perfwade her thereto; the mayde ftill refufeth. In the meane time FLAVIUS, a young man, enters in conference with the mayde, and obtaineth her confent, who being difguifed, conveyeth herfelfe away privilie with the faid FLAVIUS. Her father and PHILOTUS fearches for her in the houfe. PHILERNO, the maydes brother, laitlie arryved out of other coun- tries (being very lyke her), is miftaken, by her father and PHILOTUS, to be EMILIA, who takes the perfon of his fifter upon him; and after diverfe threatnings of his father, confentith to marrie PHILOTUS: and fo PHILOTUS committeth PHILERNO to the cuftodie of his daughter BRISILLA, untill the mariage fhould be accomplifhed. PHILERNO faines himfelfe to BRI- SILLA to be transformed. in a man, and fo maketh

B 2   himfelfe

himfelfe familiar with her. Thereafter, PHILERNO is
maried to PHILOTUS, who fearing to be difcovered,
maketh a brawling that fame night with PHILOTUS,
and abufeth him vyllie ; and to colour the mater the
better, agreeth with a whore to go to bed with PHILO-
TUS. FLAVIUS feeing the fuppofed EMILIA to bee
maried to PHILOTUS, imagines the right EMILIA to
be a devill, and, after many conjurations, expelleth
her his houfe ; fhe returneth to her father ALBERTO,
acknowledging her mifbehaviour, and lamenting her
cafe. FLAVIUS being fent for, perceiving how he had
miftaken EMILIA, revealeth the whole trueth, and fo
taketh her home agane to his wife, and PHILERNO
BRISILLA. In the end PHILOTUS bewaileth his fol-
lie, for purfuing fo unequall a match, warning all men
to beware, by his example.

AN

Ane verie excellent and delecta-
bill Treatife *, intitulit

P H I L O T U S.

PHILOTUS *directis his Speich to* EMILIE.

O Luftie luifsome lamp of licht,
Your bonynes, your bewtie bricht,
Your ftaitly ftature, trim and ticht,
   With gefture grave and gude:
Your countenance, your cullour cleir,
Your lauching lips, your fmyling cheir,
Your properties dois all appeir,
   My fenfes to illude.

2. Quhen I your bewtie do behald,
I man unto your fairnes fald:
I dow not flie howbeit I wald,
   Bot bound I man be youris:
For yow fweit hart I wald forfaik,
The Empryce for to be my maik,
Thairfoir deir dow fum pitie tak,
   And faif mee fra the fchowres.

* Comedie, ed. 1612,

t

3. Deme

3. Deme na ill of my age my dow,
Ife play the younkeris part to yow,
Firft try the treuth, then may ye trow,
    Gif I mynd to defave:
For gold nor geir ye fall not want,
Sweit hart with me thairs be na fcant,
Thairfoir fome grace unto me grant,
    For courtefie I crave.

PLESANT.   Ha, ha, quha brocht thir kittocks hither?
The mekill feind refave the fithir!
I trow ye was not al together,
    This twel-month at ane preiching.
Allace I lauch for lytill lucke,
I lauch to fie ane auld carle gucke:
*   *   *   *   *
    Fra he fall till his fleitching.

5. Now wallie as the Carle he caiges.
Gudeman quha hes maid your muftages?
Lo as the boy of fourfcoir ages,
    As he micht not be biddin:
Came ye to wow our laffe, now lachter,
Ye ar fa rafch thair will be flachter,
Ye will not fpair nor fpeir quhais aucht hir,
    Ye ar fa rafchlie riddin.

6. EMILY.   I wait not weill fir quhat ye meine,
Bot fuirlie I have feindill feine,
Ane wower of your yeirs fo keine,

    2

As ye appeir to be:
I think ane man .fir of your yeiris
Sould not be blyudit with the bleiris,
Ga feik ane partie of your peires,
    For ye get nane of mee.

The Auld Man fpeikis to the MACRELL *to allure the Madyn.*

7. Gude dame, I have yow to imploy,
Sa ye my purpofe can convoy:
And that yon laffe I micht injoy,
    Ye fould not want rewaird:
Give hir this tablet and this ring,
This purffe of gold, and fpair nathing:
Sa ye about all weill may bring,
    Of gold tak na regaird.

8. MACRELL. Na fir, let me and that allane,
Suppofe fcho war maid of a ftane,
Ife gar hir grant or all be gane,
    To be at your command:
Thocht fcho be ftrange, I think na wonder,
Blait things is fone brocht in ane blunder,
Scho is not the firft, fir, of ane hunder,
    That I have had in hand.

9. I am ane fifche, I am ane eile,
Can fteir my toung and tayle richt weill,
I give me to the mekill deill,
       B 4   Gif

Gif onie can do mair :
I can with fair anis fleitch and flatter,
And win ane crown bot with ane clatter,
That gars me drink gude wyne for watter,
   Suppois my back ga bair.

The MACRELL *intends to allure the Madyn.*

10. God blis yow Maiftres with your buik,
Leife me thay lips that I on luik :
I hope in God to fie yow bruik,
   Ane nobill houfe at hame :
I ken ane man into this toun,
Of hyeft honour and renoun,
That wald be glaid to give his gowne,
   For to have yow his dame.

11. EMILY. Now be my faull I can not fie,
That thair fik vertew is in me,
Gudwyfe, I pray yow quhat is he,
   That man quhome of ye meine?
MACRELL. PHILOTUS is the man a faith,
Ane ground-riche man, and full of graith :
He wantis na jewels, claith, nor waith,
   Bot is baith big and beine.

12. Weill war the woman all hir lyfe,
Had hap to be his weddit wyfe,
Scho micht have gold and geir als ryfe,

As copper in hir kift :
Yea, not a ladie in all this land,
I wait micht have mair wealth in hand,
Nor micht have mair at hir command,
To do with quhat fcho lift.

13. Fair floure, now fen ye may him fang,
It war not gude to let him gang,
Unto yourfelf ye'ill do greit wrang,
Sweit hart now and ye flip him :
Now thair is tweatie into this town,
Of greitift riches and renoun,
That wald be glaid for to fit doun
Upon their kneis to grip him.

14. Thocht he be auld my joy, quhat reck,
Quhen he is gane give him aue geck.
And tak another be the neck,
Quhen ye the graith have gottin :
Schaw me your mynd and quhat ye meine,
I fall convoy all this fa cleine,
That me ye fall efteme ane freine,
Quhen I am deid and rottin.

15. EMILIE. I grant gude-wyfe he is richt gude,
Ane man of wealth and nobill blude,
Bot hes mair mifter of ane hude,

And

And mittanes till his handis:
Nor of ane bairnelie lasse lyke mee,
Mair meit his oy nor wyfe to be:
His age and myne cannot agrie,
    Quhill that the warld standis.

16. MACRELL.   Let that allane, he is not sa auld,
Nor yit of curage half sa cald,
Bot gif ye war his wyfe, ye wald
    Be weill aneuch content:
With him mair treitment on ane day,
And get mair making off ye may,
Nor with ane wamsler, suith to say,
    Quhen twentie yeiris ar spent.

17. Ye neyther mell with lad nor loun,
Bot with the best in all this town,
His wyfe may ay sit formest doun,
    At eyther burde or bink :
Gang formest in at dure or yet,
And ay the first gude-day wald get,
With all men honourit and weill tret,
    As onie hart wald think.

18. Se quhat a woman's mynde may meise
And heir quhat honour, wealth, and eise,
Ye may get with him and ye pleise,

                                To

To do as I devyfe :
Your fyre fall firſt be birnand cleir,
Your madynis than fall have your geir,
Put in gude ordour and effeir,
    Ilk morning or yow ryfe.

19. And fay, lo maiſtres heir your muillis,
Put on your wylicote for it cuillis,
Lo, heir ane of your velvote ſtuillis,
    Quhairon ye fall fit doun :
Than twafum cummis to combe your hair,
Put on your heidgeir foft and fair,
Tak thair your glaſſe fie all be clair,
    And fa gais on your goun.

20. Than tak to ſtanche the * morning drouth
Ane cup of mavefie for your mouth,
For fume caſt fucker in at fouth,
    Togidder with a toiſt :
Thrie garden gowps tak of the air,
And bid your page in haiſt prepair,
For your disjone fum daintie fair,
    And cair not for na coiſt.

21. Ane pair of plevaris pypping hait,
Ane pertrick and ane quailyie get,
Ane cup of fack, fweit and weill fet,

            * your, ed. 1612.
                                        May

May for ane breckfaſt gaine.
Your cater he may cair for ſyne, , -
Sum delicate agane ye dyne,
Your cuke to ſeaſoun all ſa fyne,
 Than dois imploy his paine.

22. To ſie your ſervantes may ye gang,
And luke your madynis all amang,
And gif thair onie wark be wrang,
 Than bitterlie them blame.
Than may ye have baith quaiffis and kellis,
Hich candie ruffes and barlet bellis,
All for your weiring and not ellis,
 Maid in your houſe at hame.

23. And now quhen all thir warks is done,
For your refreſching efter none,
Gar bring unto your chalmer ſone,
 Sum danitie* diſche of meate:
Ane cup or twa with † muſcadall,
Sum uther licht thing thairwithall,
For rafins or for capers call,
 Gif that ye pleaſe to eate.

24. Till ſuppertyme then may ye chois,
Unto your garden to repois,
 Or merelie to tak ane glois,

---

* dantie, ed. 1612.   † of, ed. 1612.

 Or

Or tak ane buke and reid on ;
Syne to your fupper ar ye brocht,
Till fair full far that hes bene focht,
And daintie difches deirlie bocht,
    That ladies loves to feid on.

25. The organes than into your hall,
With fchalme and tymbrell found thay fall,
The vyole and the lute with all,
    To gar your meate difgeft :
The fupper done than up ye ryfe,
To gang ane quhyle as is the gyfe,
Be ye have rowmit ane alley thryfe,
    It is ane myle almaift.

26. Than may ye to your chalmer gang,
Begyle the nicht gif it be lang,
With talk and merie mowes amang,
    To elevate the fplene :
For your collation tak and taift,
Sum lytill licht thing till difgeft,
At nicht ufe Renfe wyne ay almaift,
    For it is cauld and clene.

27. And for your back I dar be bould,
That ye fall weir even as ye would,
With doubill garnifchings of gould,

                    And

And craip above your hair : '
Your velvote hat, your hude of ſtait,
Your myſſell quhen ye gang to gait,
Fra ſone and wind baith air and lait,
   To keip that face ſa fair.

28. Of Pareis wark wrocht by the laif,
Your fyne half-cheinyeis ye ſall have,
For to decoir ane carkat craif
   That cumlie collour bane : .
Your greit gould cheinyie for your neck,
Be bowſum to the carle and beck,
For he has gould aneuch, quhat reck?
   It will ſtand on nane.

29. And for your gownes ay the new guyſe,
Ye with your tailyeours may devyſe,
To have them louſe with plets and plyis,
   Or claſped clois behind :
The ſtuffe my hart ye neid not haine,
Pan velvot, rayſde, figurit or plaine,
Silk, ſatyne, damayſe, or grograine,
   The fyneſt ye can find.

30. Your claithes on cullouris cuttit out,
And all paſmentit round about,
My bleſſing on that femelie ſnout,

Sa weill I trow fall fet them:
Your fchankis of filk, your velvot fchone,
Your borderit wylicote abone,
As ye devyfe all fall be done,
   Uncraifit quhen ye get them.

31. Your tablet be your hals that hinges
Gould bracelets and all uther things,
And all your fingers full of rings,
   With pearls and precious ftanes:
Ye fall have ay quhill ye cry ho,
Rickillis of gould and jewellis to;
Quhat reck to tak the bogill-bo,
   My bonie burd for anis.

32. Sweit hart quhat farther wald ye have?
Quhat greiter plefour wald ye crave,
Now be my faull yow will defave,
   Your felf and ye forfaik him:
Thairfoir fweit honie I yow pray,
Tak tent in tyme and nocht delay,
Sweit fucker, nick me not with nay,
   Bot be content to tak him.

33. PLESANT. The devill cum lick that beird auld rowan.
Now fie the trottibus and trowane,
Sa bufilie as fcho is wowane,
                                        Sie

Sie as the carling craks:
Begyle the barne fho is bot young,
Foull fall thay lips, God nor that toung,
War doubill gilt with Nurifch doung,
 And ill cheir on thay cheikis.

34. EMILY. Gude-wyfe all is bot gude I heir,
For weill I lufe to mak gude cheir,
For honouris, gould, and uther geir,
 Thay can not be refufit:
I grant indeid, my daylie fair,
Will be fufficient and mair,
Bot be it gude ye do not fpair,
 As royallie to rufe it.

35. I grant all day to be weill tret,
Honours anew and hicht upfet,
But quhat intreatment fall I get,
 I pray yow in my bed?
Bot with ane lairbair for to ly,
Ane auld deid ftock, baith cauld and dry,
And all my dayes heir * I deny,
 That he my fchankes fched.

36. His eine half funken in his heid,
His lyre far caulder than the leid,
His froftie flefch as he war deid,

 * may, ed. 1611.

Will

Will for na happing heit :
Unhealthfum hoffing ever mair,
His filthfum flewme is nathing fair,
Ay rumifching with rift and rair,
　　Now, wow gif that be fweit.

37. His fkynne hard clappit to the bane,
With gut and gravell baith ovirgane,
Now quhen thir troubles hes him tane,
　　His wyfe gets all the wyte :
For Venus games I let them ga,
I geffe hee be not gude of thay ;
I could weill of his maners ma,
　　Gif I lift till indyte.

38. MACRELL. For Venus game care not a cuit,
Waill me ane wamfler that can do' it,
Sen thair may be na uther buit,
　　Plat on his head ane horne :
Handill me that with wit and fkill,
Ye may have eafments at your will,
At nicht gar young men cum yow till,
　　Put them away at morne.

39. EMILY. Gude-wyfe, all is bot vaine ye feik,
To mee of fik maters to fpeik,
Your purpois is nor worth ane leik,

　　　　　　　　I will

I will heir yow na mair:
Mark dame, and this is all and ſum,
If ever ye this earand cum,
Or of your head I heir ane mum,
  Yea ſall repent it ſair.

40. MACRELL. Yon daintie dame ſcho is ſa nyce
Sche'ill nocht be win be na devyce,
For nouther prayer nor for pryce,
  For gouid nor uther gaine.
Scho is ſa ackwart and ſa thra,
That with refuſe I come hir fra,
Scho, be Sanct Marie ſaynde mee ſa,
  I dar not ga agane.

Philotus enteris in Conference with the Madynis Father.

41. Gude goſſe, ſen ye have ever bene,
My trew and auld familiar freind,
To mak mair quentance us betwene,
  I glaidly could agrie:
Ye have ane douchter quhome untill,
I beare ane paſſing grit gude will,
Quhais phiſnomie prefigures ſkill,
  With wit and honeſtie.

42. Gif mee that laſſe to be my wyfe,
For tocher-gude ſall be na ſtryfe,
Beleive mee ſcho ſall have ane lyfe,

                                And

And for your geir I care not:
Faith ye your felf fall modifie,
Hir lyfe, rent, land, and conjunct fie,
And goffop, quhair thay fame fall be,
Appoynt the place and fpair not.

43. Betwixt us twa the heyris-maill,
Sall bruik my heritage all haill,
Quhilks gif that thay happen to faill,
To her heyris quhat faever:
My moveables I will devyde,
Ane pairt my douchter to provyde,
Ane pairt to leave fum freind afyde,
Quhen deith fall us diffever.

44. ALBERTO. Gude fir, and goffop I am glaid,
That all be done as ye have faid,
Tak baith my bliffing and the mayd,
Hame to your houfe togidder;
And gif that fcho play not hir pairt,
In onie lawfull honeft airt,
And honour yow with all hir hairt,
I wald fho gaid not thither.

ALBERTO *fpeiks to his Dochter.*

45. For the ane man I have forefeine,
Ane man of micht and welth I meine,
That ftaitlier may the fufteine,

Nor

Nor ony of all thy kin:
Ane man of honour and renoun,
Ane of the potentes of the toun;
Quhair nane may beinlier fit doun,
   This citie all within.

46. EMILY. God and gude nature dois allow,
That I obedient be to yow,
And father hithertils I trow,
   Ye have nane uther feine:
And als eftemis yow for to be,
Ane loving father unto mee,
Thairfoir deir father let mee fee,
   The man of quhome ye meine.

47. ALBERTO. PHILOTUS is the man indeid,
Quhair thow ane nobill lyfe may leid,
With quhome I did fa far proceid,
   Wee want bot thy gude will:
Now give thy frie confent thairfoir,
Deck up and do thy felf decoir,
Gang quickly to and fay no moir,
   Thow man agrie thairtill.

48. EMILIE. Gif ye fra furie wald refraine,
And patientlie heir me agane,
I fould yow fchaw in termis plane,

                                  With

With reafon ane excufe:
Sen mariage bene but thraldome free,
God and gude nature dois agree,
That I quhair as it lykes not mee,
  May lawfullie refufe.

49. I am fourtene, and hee fourefcoir,
I haill and found, hee feik and foir,
How can I give confent thairfoir,
  Or yit till him agree?
Judge gif PHILOTUS be difcreit,
To feik ane match fo far unmeit,
Thocht I refufe him father fweit,
  I pray yow pardon mee.

50. ALBERTO. How durft thow trumper be fa bald,
To tant or tell, that he was * ald?
Or durft refufe ocht that I wald
  Have biddin the obey:
Bot fen ye ftand fa lytill aw,
Ife gar yow maiftres for to knaw,
The impyre parents hes be law,
  Abuif thair children ay.

51. And heir to God I mak ane vow,
Bot gif thow at my bidding bow,
I fall the drelfe, and harkin how,

* is, ed. 1612.

C 3   And

And fyne advyfe the better:
I fall thee caft intill ane pit,
Quhair thow for yeir and day fall fit,
With breid and water furely knit
Hard bound intill ane fetter.

52. Thow fat fa foft upon thy ftuill,
That making off made the ane fuill,
Bot I fall mak thy curage cuill,
For all thy ftomack flout:
That efterwards quhill that thow leif,
Thou's be agaft mee for to greif.
Perchance thow greines that play to preif,
Advyfe thee and fpeik out.

53. EMILY. Sweit father, mitigate your rage,
Your wraith and anger, fir, affwage,
Have pitie on my youthlie age,
Your awin flefch and your blude:
Gif in your yre I be overthrawin,
Quhome have ye wraik't bot your awin,
Sik creweltie hes not bene knawin,
Amang the Turkes fa rude.

54. The favage beifts into thair kynde,
Thair young to pitie ar inclynde.
Let mercie thairfoir muif your mynde,

To

To her that humblie cryis:
Tak up and lenifie your yre,
Sufpend the furie of your fyre,
And grant me layfer, I defyre,
Ane lytill to advyfe.

*[Heir followis the Oratioun of the yonker Flavius to the
Madyn, hir anfwer and confent, the convoying of
her from her fath r: hir father and the auld wower
followis, and finds Philerno the Madyns brother laitlie
arryved, quhome thay tak to be the Madyn, and of
his deceit.*

[Flavius].

The raging low, the fcirce and flaming fyre
That dois my breift and body al combure
Incendit with the dart of grit defyre,
Fra force of thefe twa fp rking eyis ful fure,
Hes me conftraynit to cum and feik my cure
Of her, fra quhom proceidit hes my wound,
Quhom neyther falve nor fyrop can affure,
But only fho can mak me faif and found.

56. Lyke as the captive with ane tyrant taine,
Perforce with promife toifht to and fro,
Quhen that he feis all uther graces gaine,
Man fuccour fe k of him that wrocht his wo,
Sa mon I fald to my maift freindly fo,
To feik for falve of her that gave the fair:
To pray for peace, thocht rigour bid me go,
To cry for mercie, quhen as I may na mair.

57. Sa fen ye have me captivate as thrall,
Sen ye prevaill, let pitie now have place;
Have mercie fen ye maiftres ar of all,
Grudge not to grant your fupplicant fum grace.
To flay ane tain man, war bot lack allace,
Fra that he cum voluntarlie in will:
Sen I am, miftres, in the felf fame cace,
Ane thrall confenting pitie war to fpill.

58. Quhat ferly thocht, puir I with luif oppreft
Confes the force of the blynd archer boy?
How was Appollo for his Daphne dreft,
And Mars amafit his Venus to enjoy,
Did not the thundering Jupiter convoy
For Danae him felf into ane fhowre,
The gods above fen luif hath maid them coy,
Unto his law then quhy fould I not lowre?

59. As taine with ane nor Daphne mair decoir
Quhais vult to Venus may compairit be:
And bene in bewtie Danae befoir.
Suppofe the God on hir did caft his eye:
Quhais graces to hir bewtie dois agrie,
And in quhais fairnes is no toly found,
Quhat mervell miftres than, fuppofe ye fe,
With willing band me to your bewtie bound?

60. Quhais

60. Quhais bricht conteyning bewtie with the beamis
Na les al uther pulchritude dois pas
Nor to compair ane clud with glanfing gleames,
Bricht Venus cullour with ane landwart las :
The quhyteft layke bot with the blackeft affe,
The rubent rois bot with the wallowit weid ;
As pureft gold is preciouser nor glaffe,
Your bewtie fa all uther dois exceid.

61. Your hair lyk gold, and lyke the pole your eye,
Your fnawifch cheiks lyke quhyteft allabaft,
Your lovefum lip- fad, foft, and fweet-wee fie,
As rofes red quhen that ane fhowre is paft :
Your toung micht mak Demoftbenes agaft,
Your teith the peirls micht of thair place depryve
With bwillis of Indian ebur at the laft
Your papis for the prioritie dois ftryve.

62. And lyke as quhen the ftamping feale is fet
In wax weill wrocht, quhill it is foft I fay,
The prent thairof remayning may ye get,
Suppois the feale it felf be tane away,
Your femlie fhaip fa fall abyde for ay,
Quhilk throw the ficht my fenfis hes reffaifit,
Thocht abfent ye, yit I fall nicht and day,
Your prefence have as in my hart ingraifit.

63. Thocht

63. Thocht fanfie be bot * of ane figure fainit,
Nu figure feids quhair thair is na effect :
Evin fa fweit faull I perifch bot as painit,
With fanfie fed that will na fafting breck,
Suppois I have the accident quhat reck,
Grant me the folide fubftance to atteine,
Gif not, quhen ye to deith fall me direct,
Quhom bot your awin have ye confoundit clein ?

64. Laft, fen ye may my meladie remeid,
Releive your Syfiphus of his reftles ftane ;
Your pitius breift that dois full ryfely bleid,
Grant grace thairto, befoir the grip be gane,
Cum ftanche the thrift of Tantatus anone,
And cure the wounds gevin with Achilles knyfe.
Accept for yours fair maiftres, fuch a one,
That for your faik dar facrifice his lyfe.

65. EMILY. Your Orifoun, fir, foundis with fic fkil
In Cupid's court as ye had bene upbrocht :
Or fofterit in Parnaffus forkit hill
Quhair poetis hes thair flame and furie focht
Nocht taifting of fweit Helicon for nocht,
As be your plefant preface dois appeir :
Tending thairby, quhill as we have na thocht,
To mak us to your purpois to adheir.

* not, ed. 1612.

66. With

66. With loving language tending till allure,
With fweit difcourfe the fimpill till ovirfyle,
Ye caft your craft, your cunning, and your cure,
Bot puir Orphanes and Madynis to begyle,
Your waillit out words, inventit for a wyle,
To trap all thofe that trowis in yow na traine
The frute of flattrie is bot to defyle,
And fpred that wee can never get agane.

67. Ye gar us trow that all our heids be cowit,
In prayfing of our bewtie by the fkyis:
Quhen with your words we ar na mair bot mowit
This way to fie git us ye may fuppryfe,
Your doubill hart dois everie day devyfe,
Ane thowfand fhifts was never in your thocht,
Ye labour thus with all that in yow lyis,
For till undo, and bring us all to nocht.

68. And this conceat is common to yow all,
For your awin iuft, ye fet not by our fchame,
Your fweiteft word *, ar feafonit all with gall,
Your faireft phrafe, disfigures bot defame,
I think thairfoir thay gritlie ar to blame,
That trowis in yow mair nor the thing thay fe
Bot I, q hill that Emilia is my name
To trow I fall lyke to Sanct Thomas be.

* words, ed. 1612.

69. FLA-

69. FLAVIUS. For feir fweit maiftres qubat remeid?
Quha may perfwade quhair thair is dreid?
Yit deme ye wrangouflie in deid,
   Now be my faull I fweir:
Your honour, not your fchame I feik,
   count not by my luft ane leik,
It was na fik thing maiftres meik,
   That maid me to cum heir.

70. This is my fute ye fall me truft,
Judge ye your felf gif it be juft,
In honeft luif and honeft luft,
   With yow to leid my lyfe:
This is the treuth of my intent,
In lawfull lufe bot onlie bent,
Advyfe yow gif ye can confent,
   To be my weddit wyfe.

71. EMILY. Sir furelie gif I underftude,
Your meining for to be as gude,
I think in ane wee fould conclude,
   Befoir that it wer lang:
I am content to be your wyfe,
To lufe and ferve yow all my lyfe,
Bot rather flay me with a knyfe,
   Nor offer me ane wrang.

72. Bot

72. Bot Sir, ane thing I have to fay,.
My father hes this uther day.
In mariage promifit me away,
    Upon ane deid auld man ;
With quhome thocht I be not content,
Till nane uther he will confent,
Mak to thairfoir for till invent
    Ane convoy, gif yow can.

73. Lykewayis yow mon firft to me fweir,
That ye to me fall do na deir,
Nor fall not cum my bodie neir,
    For villanie nor ill :
Ay quhill the nuptiall day fall ftand,
And farther fir, gif mee' your hand,
With me for to compleit the band,
    And promeis to fulfill.

74. FLAVIUS. Have thair my hand with al my hart
And faithfull promeis for my part,
Na tyme to change quhill deithis dart,
    Put till my lyfe ane end :
Bot be ane hufband traift and trew,
For na fufpect that anis fall rew,
Bot readie ay to do my dew,
    And never till offend.

3.   75. EMILY.

75. EMILY. All day quhairto the trueth to tell,
I dar nocht with that matter mel,
Bot yit I fall devyfe my fell,
    Ane fchift to ferve our turne:
For keiping flairt baith lait and air,
Unfend-furth may I never fair,
Make I ane mint and do na mair,
    I may for ever murne.

76. Quhen I have unbethocht me thryfe,
I can na better way devyfe,
But that I man me difagyfe,
    In habite of ane man:
Thus I but danger or but dout,
This bufines may bring about,
In man's array unkend pas out,
    For ocht my keipars can.

77. Thairfoir ye fall gang and provyde,
Ane pages claithis in the meine tyde,
For all occafions me befyde,
    Againft I have ado:
Let men evin as thay lift me call,
Or quhat fumever me befall,
I hope within thrie dayis I fall,
    Cum quyetly yow to.

78. FLA-.

78. FLAVIUS. Be my awin meins I fall atteine,
And fend to yow thay claithis unfene,
Convoy lat fie all things fa tleine
    That never nane * fufpeck :
I will wait on my felf and meit yow,
To fe your new claiths as thay fet yow,
The Carle that hecht fa weill to treit yow,
    I think fall get ane geck.

79. EMILIE. I have wòn narrowlie away,
Yon Carle half put me in effray,
He lay in wait and waiting ay,
    In changing aff my claithis :
Sir, let us ga out of his ficht,
Sen I am frie, my freind gude-nicht,
He lukis as all things wer not richt,
    Lo yonder quhair he gais.

80. FLAVIUS. My onlie luif and ladie quhyte,
My darling deir and my delyte,
How fall I ever the requyte,
    This grit gude will let fee :
That, but refpect that men callis fchame,
Nor hazart of thy awin gude name,
For brute, for blafphemie nor blame,
    Hes venterit all for mee.

* never man, ed. 1612.

STEPHANO ALBERTUS SERVANT.

81. Maifter full far I have yow focht,
And full ill newes I have yow brocht,
The thing allace, I never thocht,
   Hes happinnit yow this day:
Your douchter fir (ye had bot ane)
Ane mannis claithis hes on hir tane,
And quyetlie hes hir earand gane,
   I can not tell quhat way.

82. I wonderit firft and was agaft,
Bot quhen I faw that fhe was paft
I followit efter wonder faft,
   Yit was I not the better;
Sche fchiftit hes hir felf afyde,
And in fum hous fhe did hir hyde,
Na fir, quhat ever fall betyde,
   It will be hard to get her.

83. ALBERTO. Fals pewtene hes fcho playit that fport
Hes fcho me handlit in this fort?
To God I vow cum I athort,
   And lay on hir my handis:
I fall hir ane exampill mak,
To trumpers all durft undertak,
For to commit fa foull ane fack,
   Quhill that this citie ftandis.

84. Vylde

84. Vylde vagabound, fals harlot hure,
Had sho na schame, tuke sho na cure,
Of parentis that hir gat and bure,
    Nor blude of quhilk sho sprang:
All honest bewtie to difpyfe,
And lyke ane man hir difagyfe,
Unwomanlie in fik ane wyfe,
    As gudget for to gang?

85. Fals mifchant, full of all mifcheif,
Diffaitfull traitour, commoun theif,
Of all thy kin curit not the greif,
    For flefchly foull delyte;
Quha fall into fik trumpers truft?
Quhais wickit wayis ar fa unjuft,
And led with lewd licentious luft,
    And beaftlie appetyte.

86. PHILOTUS. O fex uncertaine, frayle and fals,
Diffimulate and diffaitfull als,
With honie lips to haild in hals,
    Bot with ane wickit mynde:
Quhome will dois mair nor reafon mufe,
Mair lecherie nor honeft lufe,
Mair harlotrie nor gude behufe,
    Unconftant and unkynde.

87. In quhome ane fhaw, bot na fhame finks,
That ane rhing fayis and uther thinks:
Ane eye l ·kis up, ane uther winks,
   With fair and feinyeit face:
Bot goffop go, quhill it is greine,
For to feik out quha hes hir feine,
Gif of hir moyen wee get ane meine,
   It war ane happie grace.

88. PHILERNO. Gude firs, is nane of yow can tell,
In quhat ftreit dois Alberto dwell,
Or be quhat finge I'l knaw my fell,
   Gude brethren all about:
For thocht I be his fon and heyre,
I knaw him not a myte the mair,
And to this town dois now repair,
   My father to find out.

89. ALBERTO. Yea harlote, trowit thow for to fkip?
Sen I have gottin of the ane grip,
Be Chrift I fall thy nurture nip,
   Richt fcharply or wee fched:
For God nor I rax in ane raip
And ever thow fra my hand efcaip,
Quhill I have pullit the lyke ane paip,
   Quhair nane fall be to red.

90. PHI-

90. PHILOTUS. Rage not gude goffe, bot hald your toung.
The las bot bairnlie is and young,
I wald be laith to wit hir dung,
   Suppofe fcho hath offendit:
Forgive hir this ane fauk for mee,
And I fall fouertie for hir bee,
That inftantly fho fall agree,
   That this flip fould be mendit.

91. PHILERNO. Father I grant my haill offence,
Thir claithes I have tane till ga hence,
And gif it pleafe yow till difpence,
   With thir things that are paft:
Thir bygane faultes will ye forgive,
And efter father quhill I live,
Agane I fall yow never greive,
   Quhill that my lyfe may laft.

92. Schaw me the maner and the way,
And I your bidding fall obey,
And never fall your will gane fay,
   Bot be at your command.
ALBERTO. This fault heir frelie I forgive thee,
Philotus is the man releives thee,
Or utherwayis I had mifcheifit thee,
   And now give mee thy hand.

93. This

93 This is my ordinance and will,
Give thy confent Philotus till,
To marie him and to fulfill,
    That godlie bliffit band.
PHILERNO. Father, I hartlie am content,
And heirto gives my full confent,
For it richt fair wald mee repent,
    Gif I fould yow gainftand.

94. PHILOTUS. Heir is my hand my darling dow,
To be ane faithfull fpous to yow,
Now be my faull goffop I trow,
    This is ane happie meiting :
This matter goffe, is fa weill dreft,
That all things ar cumde for the beft,
But let us fet amang the reft,
    Ane day for all compleiting.

95. ALBERTO, Ane moneth and na langer day,
For it requyres na grit delay,
Tak thair your wyfe with yow away,
    And ufe hir as ye will.
PHILOTUS. Furfuith ye fall ga with me hame,
Quhair I fall keip yow faif fra fchame,
Unto the day, or than mee blame,
    That fcho * fall have nane ill.

* Ye. ed. 1612.

96. PLE-

96. PLESANT. Quha ever faw in all thair lyfe,
Twa cappit cairlis mak fik ane ftryfe,
To tak a young man for his wyfe,
  Yon cadgell wald be glaid:
The feind refave the feckles frunt,
*   *   *   *   *   *
The carle kennis not, he is fa blunt,
  Gif fcho be man or maid.

97. Auld guckis the mundie, fho is a gillie,
Scho is a colt-foill, not a fillie,
Scho wants a dow, bot hes a pillie,
  That will play thé ane paffe:
Put doun thy hand vane carle and graip,
As thay had wont to cheis the paip,
For thow hes gotten ane jolie jaip,
  In lykenes of ane laffe.

PHILOTUS *fpeiks to his Dochter* BRISILLA.

98. Brifilla Dochter myne give eir,
A mother I have brocht thé heir,
To mee a wyfe and darling deir,
  I thé command thairfoir,
Hir honour, ferve, obey and luif,
Wirk ay the beft for hir behuif,
To pleis hir fie thy pairt thow pruif,
  With wit and all devoir *.

    * indevoure, ed. 1612.

      D 3   PHILOTUS

Philotus to his new Bryde.

99. Ufe hir even as your awin my dow,
Keip hir, for fho fall ly with yow,
Quhill I may lawfullie avow,
   To lay yow be my fyde.
Philerno.   I fall your dochter, hufband fweit,
Na les nor my companyeoun treit,
And follow baith at bed and meit,
   Quhill that I be ane bryde.

Philerno *to* Brisilla.

100. How dois the quheill of Fortoun go,
Quhat wickit weird hes wrocht our wo?
Brisilla youris and myne alfo,
   Unhappilie, I fay:
Our fathers baith hes done agrie,
That I to youris, evin as ye fie,
And ye to myne fall maryit be,
   And all upon ane day.

101. Hard is our hap and luckles chance,
Quha pities us fuppofe wee pance?
Full oft this mater did I fkance,
   Bot with my felf befoir:
I have bene threatnit and forflittin,
Sa oft that I am with it bittin,
Invent a way or it be wittin,
   And remedie thairfoir.

I

102. Brisilla. Maiftres allace for fik remeid,
That fik ane purpois fould proceid,
I wald wifch rather to be deid.
  Nor in that manner matchit :
Quhat aillit ye parentes to prepair,
Your childrens deip continuall cair ?
Your crewell handes quhy did ye fpair,
  Firft us to have difpatchit.

103. Unnatural fathers now quhairfoir ?
Wald ye your dochters thus devoir ?
For your vane fantafies fat moir,
  Nor onie gude refpeck :
Is it not doittrie hes yow drevin,
Haiknayis to feik for haift to heavin ?
I trow that all the warld evin,
  Sall at your guckrie geck.

104. Solace to feik them felves to fla,
Ane myre to miffe thay fall in ma ;
Thay get bot greif quhen as thay ga,
  To get thair greiteft game :
And wee young things tormentit to,
Thair daffing dois us fwa undo,
Gif thay be wyfe, thair doings lo,
  Will fignifie the fame.

105. Phi-

105. PHILERNO. It profeites not for to compleine,
Let us forfie ourfelves betwene,
How wee this perrell may preveine,
    And faif us fra thair fnairis :
Gif that the goddes, as thay weill can,
Wald me transforme intill ane man,
Wee twa our felves fould marie than,
    And faif us fra thair cairis.

106. BRISILLA. Mak yow a man, that is bot mowis,
To think thairon your greif bot growis,
For that devyfe devill haid it dowis,
    Sen it can never be.
PHILERNO. Quhy not ? gif that with faith we pray
For oft the goddes as I hard fay,
Hes done the lyke and yit thay may,
    Perchance till us agrie.

107. That Iphis was a mayd we reid,
And fwa did for hir prayer fpeid,
For verie reuth the goddes indeid,
    Transformde hir in ane man :
Pigmaleon's prayer purchaft lyfe,
Unto his new eburneall wyfe,
Quhais handis had carvit hir with ane knyfe,
    With vifage paill and wan.

                                    108. Quhy

108. Quhy may not now als weill as than,
The goddes convert me in ane man,
The lyke gif that my prayer can,
    I furelie will affay :—
Maift fecreit goddes celeftiall,
Ye michtie muifers greit and fmall,
And heavinlie powers ane and all,
    Maift humblie I yow pray,

109. Luke doun from your impyre abone,
And from your heich triumphant trone,
Till us puir faullis fend fuccour fone,
    Of your maift fpeciall grace :
Behald how wee puir madynis murne,
For feir and luif how baith wee burne,
Thairfoir intill ane man mee turne,
    For till efchew this cace.

110. Behald our parents hes oppreft,
And by all dew thair dochters dreft,
With unmeit matches to moleft,
    Us fillie faullis ye fie :
Thairfoir immortall goddes of grace,
Grant that our prayeris may tak place,
Convert my kynde, this cairfull cace,
    With folace to fupplie.

111. PLE-

111. PLESANT. Ane faith perfumit with fyne folie,
And monie vane word alla-volie,
Thy prayer is not half fa holie,
  Houfe-lurdane as it femis :
Bot all inventit for a wyle,
Thy bedfallow for to begyle,
The bonie laffe bot to defyle,
  Na dowbilnes that demes.

112. BRISILLA. Maiftris quhat now? bethink ye dreme,
Or than * to be in fowne ye feime :
Scho lyis als deid, quhat fall I deime,
  Of this unhappie chance?
Scho will not heir me for na cryis,
For plucking on fcho will not ryis,
Sa lairbair-lyke lo as fcho lyis,
  As raveift in a trance.

113. PHILERNO. O blisfull deitie divyne,
Maift happie convent, court and tryne,
That dois your glorious eiris inclyne,
  Our prayeris to adheir * :
We rander thanks unto yow all,
For heiring us quhen that wee call,
And ridding us from bondage thrall,
  As plainlie dois appeir.

---

* els, ed. 1612.   † for to heare, ed. 1612.

114. I am

114. I am ane man Brisilla lo,
And with all neceffaries thairto,
May all that onie man may do,
    I fall gar yow confidder:
Now fen the goddis above hes brocht,
This wonderous wark, and hes it wrocht,
And grantit all evin as wee focht,
    Let us be glaid togidder.

115. Brisilla. Now fen the gods hes fuccour fent,·
And done even as wee did invent,
My joy I hartly am content
    To do as ye devyfe:
Throw Gods decreit my onlie choyfe,
In mutuall luif wee fall rejoyfe,
Our furious fathers baith fuppofe,
    Thay wald fkip in the fkyis.

116. Philotus. My dow fuppois I did delay,
Now cum is our fweit nuptiall day,
Thairfoir mak haift fwa that wee may,
    In tyme cum to the kirk.
Philerno. Ga quhen ye lift fir, I am readie;
Thair is ane gus-heid, for be our ladie,
I was your fone, and ye my dadie,
    This morning in the mirk.

                117. Mi-

117. MINISTER. I dout not bot ye underftand,
How God is authour of this band,
And the actioun that wee have in hand,
   He did himfelf out fet:
To that effect all men I meine,
Micht keip thair bodyes puir and cleine,
Fra fornication till abfteine,
   And children to beget.

118. Bot fen the mater cums athort,
Ilk uther day, I will be fchort,
And dois the parties baith exhort,
   To charitie and luif:
Tak heir this woman for your wyfe,
Keip, luf and cherifch hir but ftryfe,
All u her als terme of your lyfe,
   Saif hir ye fall remuif.

119. Tak for your fpous PHILOTUS than,
Obey and luif him as ye can,
Forfaik for him all uther man,
   Quhill deith do yow diffever:
The Lord to fanctifie and bleffe yow,
His grace and favour als I wifch yow,
Let not his luif and mercie miffe yow,
   Bot be with yow for ever.

                              FLA-

FLAVIUS' *conjuration.*

120. O mercie God, how may this be?
Yon is indeid richt EMILIE,
In forme of hir a faith I fie,
    Sum devill hes me defaifit:
I will in haift thairfoir gang hame,
Expell yon fpreit for fin and fchame,
And to tell me the awin richt name,
    For God's caus I will craif it.

121. The croce of God, our Saviour fweit,
To faif and fave me fra that * fpreit,
That thow na hap have for to meit,
    With me in all thy lyfe:
In God's behalf I charge the heir,
That thow ftraik in my hart na feir,
Bot pas thy way and do na deir,
    To neyther man nor wyfe.

122. Firft I conjure thé be Sanct Marie,
Be alrifch king and quene of farie,
And be the Trinitie to tarie,
    Quhill thow the treuth have taull:
Be Chrift and his apoftilles twell,
Be fanctis of hevin and hewis of hell,
Be auld Sanct Taftian * him fell,
    Be Peter and be Paull.

* thee, ed. 1612.   † Auftian, ed. 1612.

123. Be

123. Be Mathew, Mark, be Luik and Johne,
Be Lethe, Stix, and Acherone,
Be hellifche furies everie one,
   Quhair Pluto is the prince:
That thow depart and do na wonder,
Be lichtning, quhirle wind, hayle nor thunder,
That beaſt nor bodie get na blunder,
   Nor harme quhen thow gais hence.

124. Throw power I charge thé of the paip,
Thow neyther girne, gowl, glowme, nor gaip,
Lyke anker faidell, lyke unfell aip,
   Lyke owle nor alrifche elfe:
Lyke fyrie dragon full of feir,
Lyke warwolf, lyon, bull, nor beir,
Bot paſs yow hence as thow come heir,
   In lykenes of thy felfe.

125. EMILY. Gude-man quhat meine ye * ocht bot
    gude †,
Quha hes yow put in fik ane mude?
Befoir I never underſtude,
   The forme of your conjuring:
FLAVIUS. I charge thé yit as of befoir,
Pas hence and troubill me no moir,
Trowis thow to draw me ovir the fcoir,
   Fals feind with thy alluring?

* ye? ed. 1612.   † good, ed. 1612.

126. EMILY.

126. EMILY. Gude-man quhat misteris all thir mowis?
As ye war cumbred with the cowis,
Ye ar I think lyke Johne of Lowis,
   Or ane out of his minde.
FLAVIUS. In God's behalfe I the befeiche,
Impesche me not with word nor speiche,
Ill spreit, to God I me beteiche,
   Fra the and al thy kynde.

127. PLESANT. Ha ha, ha ha, ha ha, ha ha,
The feind resave the lachters a,
Quhilk is the wyseft of us twa,
   Man quhidder thow or I?
Flemit fuill, hes thow not tint thy feill,
That takis thy wyfe to be ane deill,
Thow is far vaineft I wait weill,
   Speir at the ftanders by.

128. FLAVIUS. I charge the yit as I have ellis,
Be halie relickis, beidis and bellis,
Be ermeitis that in defertis dwellis,
   Be lumitoris * and tarlochis:
Be fweit Sanct Stevin ftanit to the deid,
And be Sanct Johne his halie heid,
Be Merling, Rymour, and be Beid,
   Be witchis and be warlochis.

* limitoris, ed. 1612.

129. Be

129. Be Sanct Maloy, be Moyfes rod,
Be Mahomeir the Turkifch God,
Be Julian and Sanct Elous nod,
   Be Bernard and be Biyde :
Be Michaell that the dragon dang,
Be Gabriell and his auld fang,
Be Raphaell in tyme of thraug,
   That is to be as gyde.

130. EMILY. My luif, I think it verie lyke,
That ye war licht or lunaiyke,
Ye feir, ye fray, ye fidge, ye fyke,
   As with a fpreit poffeft :
Quhat is the mater that ye mene ?
Quhat garris yow braid ? quhair have ye bene ?
Quhat aillis yow joy ? quhat have ye fene ?
   To rage with fik unreft.

131. FLAVIUS. Quhat have I fene fals hound of hell,
I trowit quhen I did with the mell,
Thow was richt EMILIE thy fell
   Not ane incarnate devill :
Bot I richt now with my awin eine,
Richt EMILIE have maryit feine,
Sa thow mon be ane fpreit uncleine,
   Lord faif me fra thy evill.

132. Be

132. Be vertew of the Halie Ghaift,
Depairt out of myne hous in haift,
And God quhais power and micht is maift,
   Conferve me fra thy cummer:
Gang hence to hell or to the farie,
With me thow ma na langer tarie,
For quhy? I fweir the be Sanct Marie,
   Thou's be nane of my nummer.

133. PHILERNO. Gar wfche this hous for it grows lait.
Hufband I have for to debait,
With yow a lytill of eftait,
   Befoir wee go to bed:
Sen I am young and ye ar auld,
My curage kene, and ye bot cauld,
The ane mon to the uther fauld,
   A faith befoir we fched.

134. PHILOTUS. We wil not for the maiftrie ftryve,
We mon grie better and we thryve.
PHILERNO. Na be my faull we' is wit belyve,
   Quha gets the upper hand:
Indeid thow fall beir mee a bevell,
For with my neives I fall the navell;
Auld cuftrone carle tak thair a revell,
   Than do as I command.

VOL. III.   É   135. PHI-

135. PHILOTUS. I fie it cummis to cuffis the'man,
Ile end the play that thow began,
That victorie thow never wan,
    That fall be bocht fa deir:
Ha mercie, mercie EMILIE,
Tak ye the maiftrie all for me,
For I fall at your bidding be,
    And flay me not, I fweir.

136. PLESANT. Wel clappit burd quhan wil ye kiffe?
Auld fuill, the feind refave the miffe,
Ye trowit to get ane burd of bliffe,
    To have ane of thir maggies:
Quhat think ye now? how is the cace,
Now ye'ill all doit *, allace, allace,
Now grace and honour on that face,
    ' Quod Robein to the haggies.

137. PHILERNO. Than hecht in haift thairfoir that thow
Sall readie at my bidding bow,
Quhat ever I do thow fall allow,
    My fanfie to fulfill:
Sa gang I out, fa cum I in,
Sa gif I waift, fa gif I win,
Quhat ever I do mak ye na din,
    Bot let me wirk my will.

* ye'ill do it all, ed. 1612.

138. Thou

138. Thou may not fpeir the caus, and quhy,
Quhen that I lift not with yow ly,
Quhat I the bid, and thow deny,
  Wee will not weill agrie:
Quhen that I pleis furth to repair
Speir not the cumpanie, nor quhair:
Content thyfelf and mak na mair,
  I man thy maifter be.

139. PHILOTUS. I am content quhen and how fone,
All till obey that ye injone,
That ye command it man be done
  Thair is nane uther buit.
PHILERNO. Quhat is your pryce damefall fair?
Quhat tak ye for a nichts lair?
HUIR. Ye fall a crown upon me fpair,
  Bot quhom with fal I do it?

140. PHILERNO. Ile get a man, have heir a croun,
Bot be weill ftrange quhen ye ly doun,
Mak nyce and gar the larbair lowne,
  Beleve ye be a mayd.
HUIR. The youngeft las in all this citie,
Sall byde na mair requeift nor treitie,
Ile cry as I war huirt for pitie,
  Quhen I am with him laid.

141. EMILY. Now fen my hufband hes done fa,
But caus for to put me him fra,
I will unto my father ga,
    Befoir his feit to fald.
Father fa far I did offend,
That I may not my mis amend,
And am ovir pert for to pretend
    Your dochter to be cald.

142. ALBERTO. Lament not, let that mater be,
Thy faltis ar buriet all with me.
Betwixt thy hufband now and thee,
    Is onie new debait?
EMILY. I knaw of nane, bot hee indeid
Hes put mee fra him, quhat remeid?
And will na mair fik fofteris feid,
    He fayis of myne eftait.

143. ALBERTO. Quhat is the mater that ye meine
Againft all ordour clair and cleine,
Schut hame your wyfe that hes not bene,
    Yit fyve dayes in your aucht:
Is this ane plefant godlie lyfe,
To be in barrace, fturt and ftryfe,
The feind wald faine man be your wyfe,
    Can never fit in faucht.

144. PHI-

144. PHILOTUS. Knew ye the treuth gude-man I trow
Hir labour ye fould not allow,
Luke all my face, behald my brow,
  That is baith blak and bla.
ALBERTO. It may weill be, I can not tell,
That fcho durft with that mater mell,
Let hir mak anfwer for hir fell,
  To fie gif it be fa.

145. Dochter gave I the this command,
That thow thy hufband fould ganeftand,
How durft thow huir, him with thy hand,
  Put to the point of felling.
EMILY. That war grit wrang fir, gif fa bee,
Bot hee na hufband is to mee,
Than how could wee twa difagree,
  That never had na melling ?

146. ALBERTO. Na melling miftris ? wil ye than
Deny the mariage of that man,
In face of halie kirk quha can,
  This open deid deny ?
EMILY. Let refoun fir with yow prevaill,
Condemne mee not firft in the faill,
Befoir that ye have hard my taill,
  The treuth fyne* may ye try.

* then, ed. 1612.
E 3   147. Now

147. Now this is all that I wald say,
That FLAVIUS tuke mee away,
About a moneth and a day,
   Dreft in a varlet's weid:
With quhome I have bene ever ftill,
Ane uther EMILIE ay and quhill,
Hee faw yow give PHILOTUS till,
   And than in verie deid,

148. Supponing mee ane devill of hell,
With crewell conjuratiounes fell,
Did mee out of his hous expell,
   As with a bogill bazed:
As ane out of his mynde or marrit,
He hes mee of his hous debarrit,
I can not tell quhat hes him fkarrit,
   Or hes the man amazed.

149. ALBERTO. This purpois goffe, appeirs to me
Sa wonder nyce and ftrange to be,
That wee to wit the veritie,
   For FLAVIUS man fend;
Sir gif ye could declair us now,
How lang this woman was with yow,
And all the maner quhen and how,
   Wee wald richt gladlie kend.

150. FLA-

150. FLAVIUS. Sa far ALBERTO as I knaw,
I fall the fuith unto you fchaw,
Quhen I your douchters bewtie I faw *,
  I offerit hir gude-will:
Accepting than the promife maid,
Cled lyke a boy but mair abaid,
Fra yow diffaitfullie fcho flaid,
  And come myne houfe untill.

151. Quhair I hir keipit as my wyfe,
Tret, luifit and chereift hir for lyfe,
Quhill efter-ward fell out ane ftryfe,
  Thir maters all amang:
For plainlie in the kirk I faw,
This man became your fone in law,
I did thairfoir perfytly knaw,
  My EMILIE was wrang.

152. And that fome fpreit hir fchaip had tane
Sen EMILIES thair was bot ane,
I thairfoir to that ghaift have gane,
  Conjuring hir my fell:
And fra my hous expellit hir to,
This woman feimis for to be fcho,
Senfyne I had na mair ado,
  With that fals feind of hell.

* bewtie faw, ed. 1612.
E 4   153. PHI-

153. PHILOTUS. Now FLAVIUS, I wait richt weil
Sen ane of them man be a deill,
My maiglit face maks me to feill,
    That myne man be the fame:
For quhy: richt EMILIE is youris,
And that incarnate devill is ouris,
I gat, ye may fie be my clouris,
    A deill unto my dame.

154. PHILERNO. Heir I am cum to red the ftryfe,
For I am neytier deill nor wyfe,
Bot am ane young man be my lyfe,
    Your fone, fir, and your air;
Quhome ye for EMILIE haif tane,
And wald not firs let mee allane,
Quhill ye faw quhat gait it is gane,
    I can tell yow na mair.

155. PHILOTUS. A man, allace, and harmifay,
That with my only dochter lay,
Syne dang my fell: quhat fall I fay
    Of this unhappie chance?
Have I not maid a berrie block,
That hes for Jennie maryit Jock?
That mowit my dochter for a mock,
    The devill be at the dance.

                           156. Allace

156. Allace, I am for ever fchamit,
To be thus in my eild defamit,
My dochter is not to be blamit,
  For I had all the wyte :
Auld men is twyfe bairnis, I perfaif,
The wyfeft will in wowing raif
I for my labour with the laif,
  Am drivin to this difpyte.

157. ALBERTO. Gude goffe, your wraith to pacifie,
Sen that thair may na better bee,
I am content my fone that hee
  Sall with your dochter marie.
PHILERNO. I am content with hart and will,
This mariage father to fulfill,
Quhat neidis PHILOTUS to think ill,
  Or yit his weird to warie.

158. FLAVIUS. Be frolick FLAVIUS and faine,
To get thy EMILIE againe.
To deme my dow, was I not vaine,
  That thow had bene a fpreit?
Now fen I am fred fra that feir,
And vaine illufioun did appeir,
Welcum my darling and my deir,
  My fucker and my fweit.

159. Gude

159. Gude firs, quhat is thair mair ado
Ilk youth his lufe hes gotten lo,
Let us thairfoir go quicklie to,
   And marie with our maitis:
Let us foure lufers now rejoyfe,
Ilk ane for to injoy his choyfe,
Ane meiter matche nor ane of thofe,
   For tender young eftaitis.

160. Let us all foure now with ane fang*,
With mirth and melodie amang,
Give gloir to God that in this thrang,
   Hes bene all our releif:
That hes fra thraldome fet us frie,   ·
And hes us placit in fik degrie,
Ilk ane as hee wald wifch to be,
   With glaidnes for his greif.

Ane Sang of the Foure Lufearis.

Were Jacob's fones mair joyfull for to fe,
The waltring wawes King Pharaoh's oift confound,
Was Ifrael mair glaid in hart to be
Fred from all feir, befoir in bondage bound?
Quhen God them brocht from the Egiptian ground,
Was Mordocheus merier nor wee,
Quhen Artaxerxes alterit his decrie?

   * Let us foure now all with one fong, ed. 1612.

162. Was

162. Was greiter glaidnes in the land of Greice
Quhen Jaſon come from Colchos hame agane
And conqueiſt had the famous golden fleis;
With labour lang, with perrell and with pane?
The father Æzon was not half ſa faine,
To ſie his ſone returning with ſik gloir,
As wee, quhais myndis ar ſatisfyit, and moir.

163. Gif onie joy into this earth belaw,
Or warldlie p'eſour reput be perſyte,
Quhat greiter ſolace ſall ye to mee ſhaw,
Nor till injoy your hartis all haill delyte?
To have your lufe and luſtie ladie quhyte,
In quhome ye may baith nicht and day rejoyfe:
In quhome ye may your pleſures all repoſe.

164. Let us thairfoir, ſen evin as wee wald wiſſe,
Reciprocklie with leill and mutuall lufe,
As fleitand in the fludes of joy and bliſſe,
With ſolace ſing and ſorrowes all remufe,
Let us the fructes of preſent pleſour pruſe,
In recompence of all our former pane,
And miſerie, quhairin wee did remane.

PHILOTUS.

165. Bot now advert gude bretherin all about,
That of my labour hes the ſucces ſeine:
Ye that hes hard this haill diſcourſe throw out,
May knaw how far that I abuſit have bene,

I grant

I grant indeid thair will na man me meine,
For I my felf am authour of my greif,
That by my calling fould be caryit cleine,
With youthlie toyis unto fa greit mifcheif.

166. Gif I had weyit my gravitie and age,
Rememberit als my firft and auncient fait,
I had not fowmit in fik unkyndlie rage,
For to difgrace mine honour and eftait,
Quhat had bocht bot to my felf debait,
Suppois the mater had cum than as I meinit:
Nay my repentance is not half fa lait,
As I had gotin the thing quhairfoir I greinit.

167. For thocht my folie did the Lord offend,
Yit my gude God hes wrocht all for the beft ;
And this rebuik hes thairfoir to me fend,
All fik inordinate doings to deteft,
Quhilk fweit rebuik I reckin with the reft,
From fatherlie affection to proceid,
That uthers with lyke paffiouns poffeft,
May leirne be my exampill to tak heid.

168. Sen age thairfoir fuld governit be with fkill,
Let countenance accord with your gray hairis ;
Ye auncients all, let refoun rewll your will,
Subdew your fenfis till efchew thir fnairis,

Gif

Gif ye wald not incombred be with cairis,
Be maifter over your awin affections haill:
For hailillie * the praife is onlie thairs,
That may againft fik paffions prevaill.

The Meffinger.

169. Gude firs, now have ye hard and fene this ferfe †,
Unworthie of your audience I grant,
Unformallie fet out in vulgar verfe,
Of waillit out words and leirnit leid bot fkant ‡.
The courteours that princes hallis do hant,
I wait will never for my rudenes rufe mee:
Yit my gude·will for to fupplie the want,
I hope fall of your courtefies excufe mee.

170. For paffing well I have imployit my panis
Swa that ye can be with the fame content:
For dew regaird gude acceptiouns gaines,
And parties pleifit dois mak the tyme wel fpent.
Gif God had greiter leirning to mee lent,
I fuld have fchawin the fame with als gude will:
Wyte ignorance that I did not invent,
Ane ferfe that micht your fantafies fulfill.

* wholie all, ed. 1612.
† have ye heard us here reherfe, ed. 1612.
‡ language fkant, ed. 1612.

5   171. Laſt

171. Laſt firs, now let us pray with ane accord *,
For to preſerve the perſoun of our king :
Accounting ay this gift as of the Lord,
Ane prudent Prince above us for to ring.
Than gloir to God, and prayſis let us ſing,
The Father, Sone, and Halie Gaiſt our gyde,
Of his mercies us to conduct and bring,
To hevin for ay in pleſoures to abyde.

F I N I S.

[S O N G†.]

What if a day or a month or a yeere
Crown thy deſire with a thouſand wiſched contentings ;
Can not the chance of ane nicht or ane houre,
Croſſe thy delightes with a thowſand ſad tormentings ?
Fortune, honour, beutie, youth, are but bloſſomes dying,
Wanton pleſoures, dotting love, are but ſhadowes flying :
All our joyes are but toyes idle thoughtes deceaving,
None hes power of an houre in thair lyves bereaving.

* Laſt let us pray to God with one accord, ed. 1612.
† From hence to the end omitted in the ed. of 1612.

Earth's but a point of the world, and a man
Is but a poynt of the earth's compared centure.
Shall than the poynt of a poynt be so vaine
As to delight in a sillie poynts aventure ?
All is hazard that wee have, here is nothing byding :
Dayes of pleasures ar but stremes throgh fair medowes
  glyding.
Well or wo tyme dois go, in tyme is no returning,
Secreete fates guydes our states, both in mirth and murning.

GAWAN.

GAWAN AND GOLOGRAS.

A METRICAL ROMANCE.

From the Edition printed at Edinburgh 1508, 8vo.

*** The divifion into Parts, and the Arguments, are not in the original Impreffion.

VOL. III.   F   GAWAN

GAWAN and GOLOGRAS.

PART I.

ARGUMENT.

KING ARTHUR goes to the Holy Land by Tufcany or Italy, and his fplendid attendance, St. 1. 11.—Difficulties of the way, 111.—Difcover a city and caftle, 1v.—Sir KAY fent to examine, and enters a hall, v.—Hall defcribed: Sir KAY fees a fire, vi.—Sir KAY takes meat from the fpits, and a knight appears, vii.—The knight blames KAY, who retorts, viii.—KAY knocked down, and rides back to ARTHUR, ix.—GAWAN fent, x.—GAWAN begs the lord of the caftle for victuals for price, xi.—The lord fays all is ARTHUR's own, and blames KAY, xii, xiii.—GAWAN returns to ARTHUR, who goes to the caftle, xiv.—The lord offers

F 2   all

all to ARTHUR, and fays he is his coufin, xv, xvi.—
Entertainment for four days: ARTHUR proceeds: hunting, and journey, xvii, xviii.—They fee a caftle on
the river Rhone, which afterward proves to be that of
GOLOGRAS, xix.—ARTHUR enquires who is lord,
xx.—SPINAGROS fays, a knight who owns no fuperior.
ARTHUR vows that he will fubdue him at his return,
xxi.—SPINAGROS anfwers, that even the King of
Macedon did not fubdue him, xxii.—ARTHUR infifts
on his vow, xxiii.—Goes to Jerufalem by fea, and
returns to the Rhone, xxiv.

I.

IN the tyme of ARTHUR, as trew men me tald,
The king turnit ou ane tyde towart *Tufkane*;
Hym to feik our the fey, that faikles wes fald,
The fyre that fendis all feill futhlie tc fane.
With banrentis, baronis, and bernis fu l bald,
Biggaft of bane and blude, bred in *Britane*.
Thai walit out worryouris, with wapinnis to wald;
The gayeft grumys on grund with geir that mycht gane.
Dukis and digne lordis, douchty and deir,
Sembillit to his fummoune;
Renkis of grete renoune;
Cumly kingis, with croune
Of gold that wes cleir.

II.

Thus the Royale can remove, with his round tabill,
Of all riches maift rike, in riall array;
Was never fundun on fold, but fenyeing or fabill,
Ane farayr floure on ane field, of frefch men in fay,
Farand on thair ftedis ftout men and ftabill;
Mony fterne our the ftreit ftertis on ftray.
Thair baneris fchane with the fone, of filver and fabill,
And uther glemyt as gold, and gowlis fo gay.
Of filver and faphir fchirly thai fchane ;
Ane fair battel on breid,
Merkit our ane fair meid.
With fpurris fpedely thai fpeid
Our fellis in fane.

III.

The king faris with his folk, our firthis and fellis,
Feill dais or he fand of flynd or of fyre;
Bot deip dalis bedene, dounis, and dellis,
Montains, and mareffe, with mony rank myre;
Birk in bewis, about boggis and wellis;
Withoutin beilding of blis, of bern, or of byre:
Bot torris, and tene wais, teirfull quha tellis,
Tuglit and travalit thus trew men can tyre.
Sa wundir wait wes the way, wit ye but wene.
And all thair vittalis war gone,
That thay weildit in wone.
Reffet couth thai find none
That fuld thair bute ben.

IV. As

IV.

As thay walkit be the fyde of ane fair well,
Throu the fchynyng of the fon ane cieté thai fe.
With torris, and turatis, teirfull to tell,
Bigly batollit about with wallis fa he.
The yettis war clenely kepit with ane caftell,
Myght none fang it with force, bot foullis to fle.
Than carpit King ARTHUR, kene and cruel,
" I rede we fend furth ane fend to yone cieté,
" And afk leif at the lord yone lands fuld leid,
" That we myght entir in his toune,
" For his hie renoune,
" To by us vittale boune,
" For money to meid·"

V.

Schir KAY carpit to the king courtes and cleir,
" Grant me, lord, on yone gait graithly to gay,
" And I fall boidword, but abaid, bring to you heir,
" Gif he be frick on the fold, your freynd, or your fay."
' Sen thi will is to wend, wy, now in weir,
' Luke that wifly thow wirk. Crifte were thé fra wa!'
The herne bounit to the burgh, with ane blith cheir,
Fand the yettis unclofit, and thrang in fell thra.
His hors he tyit to ane tre treuly that tyde.
Syne hynt to ane hie hall,
That wes aftalit with pall;
Weill wro‿ht wes the wall,
And payntit with pride.

VI. The

VI.

The fylour deir of the deife dayntely wes dent
With the doughtyeft, in thair dais, dyntis couth dele,
Bright letteris of gold, blith unto blent,
Makand mencioune quha maift of manhede couth mele.
He faw nane levand leid upone loft lent,
Nouthir lord, na lad; 'leif ye the lele.
The renk raikit in the faill, riale and gent,
That wondir wifly wes wroght, with wourfchip and wele.
The berne befely and bane blinkit hym about:
He faw, throu ane entré,
Charcole in ane chymné;
Ane bright fyre couth he fe,
Birnand full ftout.

VII.

Ane Duergh braydit about, befily and bane,
Small birdis on broche, be ane brigh fyre.
Schir KAY rufchit to the roift, and reft fra the fwane;
Lightly claught, throu luft, the lym fra the lyre.
To feid him of that fyne fude the freik wes full fane.
Than dynnyt the Duergh in angir and yre,
With raris quhil the rude hall reirdit agane.
With that come girdand in greif ane wound grym Sire.
With ftout contenance and fture he ftude thame beforne;
With vefage lufly and lang,
Body ftalwart and ftrang,
That fege wald fit with none wrang
Of berne that wes borne.

F 4   VIII. The

VIII.

The knyght carpit to Schir KAY, cruel and kene,
" Methink thow fedis thé unfair, freik, be my fay!
" Suppofe thi birny be bright, as bachiler fuld ben,
" Yhit ar thi latis unlufsum, and ladlike, I lay.
" Quhy has thou marrit my man with maiftri to mene ?
" Bot thow mend hym that mys, be Mary, mylde may,
" Thow fall rew in thi rufe, wit thow but wene,
" Or thow wond of this wane wemeles away."
Schir KAY wes haifty, and hate, and of ane hie will.
Spedely to hym fpak,
" Schort amendis will I mak.
" Thi fchore compt I noght ane laik :
" Traift wele thair till."

IX.

Thair with the grume in his grief leit gird to Schir KAY;
Fellit the freke with his fift flat in the flure.
He wes fa aftonayt with the ftraik, in ftede qubare he lay
Stok ftill as ane ftane; the fterne wes fa fture.
The freik na forthir he faris, bot foundis away.
The tothir drew hym on dieigh in derne to the dure;
Hyit hym hard throu the hall to his haiknay,
And fped hym on fpedely, on the fpare mure,
The renk reftles he raid to ARTHOUR the king.
Said, " lord wendis in your way:
" Yone berne nykis you with nay.
" To prife hym forthir to pray
" It helpis na thing."

X. Than

X.

Than fpak Schir GAWANE the gay, gratious and gude,
" Schir ye knaw that Schir KAY is crabbit of kynde. .
" I rede ye mak furth ane man mekar of mude,
" That will with fairnes fraift frendfchip to fynd.
" Your folk ar febil, and faynt, for falt of thair fude." .
' Sum better boidword to abide, undir wod lynd,
' Schir GAWYNE, graith ye that gait, for the gude rude;
' Is nane fa bowfum ane berne, brith for to bynd.'
The heynd knight at his haift held to the toune.
The yettis wappit war wyde
The knyght can raithly in ryde.
Reynit his palfray of pryde,
Quhen he ves lighit doun.

XI.

Schir GAWYNE gais furth the gait that graithit wes gay,
The quhilk that held to the hall, heyndly to fe.
Than wes the Syre in the faill, with renkis of array,
And blith birdis hym about, that bright wes of ble.
Wourtby Schir GAWYNE went on his way :
Sobirly the foverane faluft has he.
" I am fend to your felf, and charge for to fay,
" Fra cumly ARTHUR the king, corteffe and fre.
" Quhilk prays for his faik and your gentrice,
" That he might cum this toun till,
" To by vittale at will,
" Alfe deir as fegis will fell,
" Payand the price."

XII. Than

XII.

Than fayd the fyre of the faill, and the foverane,
" I will na vittale be fauld your fenyeour untill."
" That is at your aune will," faid wourthy GAWANE.
" To mak you lord of your aune methink it grete fkill."
Than right gudly that grome anfuerit agane,
" Quhy I tell thé this taill, tak tent now thair till.
" Pafe on thi purpos, furth to the plane:
" For all the wyis I weild ar at his aune wil',
" How to luge, and to leynd, and in my land lent.
" Gif I fauld hym his awin,
" It war wrang to be knawin:
" Than war I wourthy to be drawin
" Baldly on bent.

XIII.

" 'I hare come ane laithles leidair to this place,
" With ane girdill ourgilt, and uthir light gere.
" It kythit, be his cognifance, ane knight that he wes;
" But he wes ladlike of lait, and light of his feré.
" The verray caufe of his come I knew noght the cace,
" But wondir wraighly he wroght, and all as of were.
" Yit wait I noght quhat he is, be Goddis grete grace:
" But gif it happin that he be ane knyght of youris here,
" Has done my lord to difpleife, that I hym faid ryght,
" And his prefence plane;
" I fay you in certane
" He fal be fet agane,
" As I am trew knight."

XIV. Schir

XIV.

Schir GAWINE gettis his leif, and grathis to his steid ;
And broght to the bauld king boidword of blis.
" Weill gretis yow, lord, yone lusty in leid,
" Ard says him likis in land your langour to lis.
" All the wyis in welth he weildis in weid
" Sall halely be at your will, all that is his."
Than he merkit with myrth, our ane grene meid,
With all the best, to the burgh, of lordis I wis.
The knight kepit the king, cumly and cleir,
With lordis and ladyis of estate,
Met hym furth on the gate,
Syne tuke hym in at yate
With ane bligh cheir.

XV.

He had that heynd to ane hall, hiely on hight,
With dukes and digne lordis, doughty indeid.
" Ye ar welcum, cumly king," said the kene knyght,
" Ay quhil yow likis, and list, to luge in this leid.
" Heir I mak yow of myne maister of myght,
" Of all the wyis, and welth, I weild in this steid,
" Thair is na ridand Roy, be refoun and right,
" Sa deir welcum this day, doutles but dreid.
" I am your coufing of kyn, I mak to you knawin.
" This kyth, and this castell,
" Firth, forest, and fell,
" Ay quhill you likis to duell,
" Ressave as your awin.

XVI. " I may

XVI.

" I may refrefch you with folk to feght, gif you nedis,
" With thretty thoufand tald, and traiftfully tight,
" Of wife, wourthy, and wight, in thair were wedis;
" Baith with birny, and brand, to ftrenth you ful ftright,
" Weill ftuffit in fteill, on thair ftout ftedis."
Than faid King ARTHUR hymfelf, feymly be fight,
" Sic frepdfchip I hald fair, that forffis thair dedis;
" Thi kyndnes fal be quyt, as I am trew knight."
Than thay bufkit to the bynke, beirnis of the beft;
The king crounit with gold;
Dukis deir to behold;
Allyns the banrent bold
Gladdit his geft.

XVII.

Thair myght feruice be fene, with fegis in faill,
Thoght all felcought war foght, fra the fon to the fee.
Wynis went within the wane, maift wourthy to waill
In coupis of cleir gold, brichteft of blee.
It was full teir to tell, treuly in taill,
The feir courffis that war fet in that femblee.
The mercift war menfkit on mete at the maill,
With menftralis myrthfully makand thame glee.
'Thus thay folaift thame felvin, futhly to fay
Al thay four dais to end.
The king thankit the heynd;
Syne tuke his leve for to wend;
And went on his way.

XVIII. Thus

XVIII.

Thus refrefchit he his folk, in grete fufioun ;
Withoutin wanting in waill, waftell, or wyne.
Thai turffit up tentis, and turnit of toun,
The Roy with his round tabill, richeft of ryne.
Thay drive on the da deir, be dalis and doun,
And of the nobilleft be name noumerit of nyne.
Quhen it drew to the dirk nycht, and the day yeid doun,
Thai plantit doun pavillonis proudly fra thine.
Thus journait gentilly thyr chevalroufe knichtis
Ithandly ilk day,
Throu mony fer contray,
Our the montains gay,
Holtis, and hillis.

XIX.

Thai paffit in thare pilgrimage, the proudeft in pal,
The prince provit in prefe, that prife wes and deir.
Syne war thai war of ane wane, wrocht with ane wal,
Reirdit on ane riche roche, befide ane riveir.
With doubill dykis bedene, drawin our all ;
Micht nane thame note with invy, nor nycht thame to neir.
The land was likand in large, and lufsom to call.
Propir fchene fchane the fon, reymly and feir.
The king ftude vefiand the wall, maift vailyeand to fe.
On that river he faw
Cumly touris to knaw :
The Roy rekinnit on raw
Thretty and thre.

XX. Apone

XX.

Apone that riche river, randonit full evin,
The fide wallis war fet, fad to the fee.
Scippis faland thame by, fexty and fevyn,
To fend, quhen thamefelf lift, in fcir cuntré:
That all thai that ar wrocht, undir the hie hevin,
Micht nocht warne thame, at will, to ifche, nor entré.
Than carpit the cumly king, with ane loud ftevin,
‘ Yone is the feymliaft ficht, that ever couth I fe !
‘ Gif thair be any keyne knycht that can tell it,
‘ Quha is lord of yone land,
‘ Lufty and likand ;
‘ Or quham of is he haldand;
‘ Fayne wald I wit.’

XXI.

Than Schir SPYNAGROSE with fpeche fpak to the king,
“ Yone lord haldis of nane leid that yone land aw ;
“ Bot ever lefting, but legiance, to his leving,
“ As his eldaris has done, enduring his daw.”
‘ Hevinly God,’ faid the heynd; ‘how happy nis this thing?
‘ Herd thair ever ony fage fa felcouth ane faw ?
‘ Sal never myne hart be in faill, na in liking,
‘ Bot gif I loiffing my life, or be laid law,
‘ Be the pilgramage compleit, 1 pas for faull-prow ;
‘ Bot dede be my deftenyng,
‘ He fall, at my agane cumyng,
‘ Mak homage and obliffing,
‘ I mak myne avow.’

XXII. “ A

XXII.

" A Lord! fparis of fic fpeche, quhill ye fpeir more;
" For abandonit will he noght be, to berne that is borne;
" Or he be ftrenyeit with ftrenth, youe fterne for to fchore,
" Mony ledis fal be loiffit, and liffis forlorne.
" Spekis na fucceudry, for Criftis fone deir.
" Yone knicht to fcar wyth fkaith ye chaip nocht but fcorne.
" It is full fair for to be fallow, and feir,
" To the beft that has been beevit you beforne.
" The myghty King of *Maffidone*, wourthieft but wene,
" Thair gat he nane homage,
" For all his hie parage,
" Of lord of yone lyuage,
" Nor never none fene.

XXIII.

" The wy that wendis for to were quhen he wenys beft,
" All his will in this warld with welthis, I wys,
" Yit fall be licht as leif of the lynd left,
" That welters down with the wynd, fa waverand it is.
" Your mycht and your majefté mefure but mys."
' In faith,' faid the cumly king, ' throw the full traift
' My hecht fall haldin be, for bail or for blis.
' Sall never my likame be laid unlaiffit to fleip,
' Quhill I have gart yone berne bow,
' As I have maid myne avow.
' Or ellis mony wedou
' Full wraithly fall weip.'

XXIV. Thair

XXIV.

Thair wes na man that durſt mel to the king,
Quhan thai ſaw that mighty ſa movit in his mude.
The Roy rial raid, withoutin reſting,
And ſocht to the *ciete of Criſte*, our the ſalt flude.
With mekil honour in erd he maid his offering.
Syne buſkit hame the ſamyne way, that he before yude.
Thayr wes na ſpurris to ſpair, ſpedely thai ſpring ;
Thai brochit bloukis to thair ſidis briſt of rede blude.
Thus the Roy, and his rout, reſtles thai raid
Ithandly ilk day,
Our the montains gay,
To *Rone* * tuke the reddy way,
Withoutin mare abaid.

---

* The river Rhone.   Part IV. St. 27.

PART II.

PART II.

ARGUMENT.

ARTHUR plants his pavilions before the castle of Golo-
gras, I.—Advised to send an envoy, II.—SPINA-
GROS praises the Lord of the Castle, and advises mild-
ness, III. IV.—Envoys sent and salute the Lord, V, VI.
GAWAN delivers the message to GOLOGRAS, VII,
VIII, IX.—GOLOGRAS refuses homage, X, XI.—
The preparations and siege, XII, XIII, XIV.—ARTHUR
insists, SPINAGROS praises GOLOGRAS, XV, XVI.—
ARTHUR hears a signal and GALIOT comes to chal-
lenge, XVII, XVIII.—ARTHUR calls GAUDIFER to
fight him, XIX.—Who takes GALIOT prisoner, XX,
XXI.—Grief of GOLOGRAS, who sends Sir RIGAL of
RHONE, XXII.—RANALD fights him: both killed,
XXIII, XXIV, XXV, XXVI.

I.

Thai plantit doun ane pailyeoun, upon ane plane lee,
Of pall and of pillour that proudly wes picht ;
With rapis of rede gold, riale to fee,
And grete enfenyes of the famyne femly by ficht.
Bourdouris about, that bricht war of ble,
Betin with brint gold, burely and bricht ;
Frenyeis of fyne filk fretitt full fre,
With deir dyamonthis bedene, that dayntely wes dicht.
The king cumly in kith, coverit with croune,
Callit knichtis fa kene,
Dukis douchty bedene :
" I rede we caft us betuene
" How beft is to done.

II.

Than fpak ane wight werior, wourthy and wife,
" I rede ane fayndis man ye fend to yone fenyeour,
" Of the proudeft in pall, and haldin of prife,
" Wife, vailyeing, and moift of valour.
" Gif yone douchty in deid will do your devife,
" Be boune at your bidding, in burgh and in bour,
" Reffave him reverendly, as refoun in lyis ;
" And gif he nykis you with nay, you worthis on neid
" For to affege yone caftel,
" With cant men and cruel,
" Durandly for to duel,
" Ever quhill you fpeid."

5   III. Than

III.

Than fchir GAVANE the gay, grété of degre,
And Schir LANCELOT DE LAKE, withoutin lefing,
And avenand Schir EWIN thai ordanit ; that thre
To the fchore Chiftane chargit fra the kyng. ·
SPYNAGROS than fpekis ; faid, " Lordingis in le,
" I rede ye tent trewly to my teching,
" For I knaw yone bauld berne better than ye ;
" His land, and his lordfchip, and his leving.
" And ye ar thre in this thede thrivand oft in thrang ;
" War al your ftrenthis in ane,
" In his grippis and ye gane,
" He wald ourcum you ilk ane ;
" Yone fterne is fa ftrang.

IV.

" And he is maid on mold meik as ane child ;
" Blith and boufum that berne, as byrd in hir bour.
" Fayr of fell, and of face, as flour unfild :
" Wondir ftalwart, and ftrang, to ftrive in ane ftour.
" Thairfore meikly with mouth mel to that myld,
" And make him na manance, bot all mefoure.
" Thus with trety ye caft yon trew undre tyld,
" And faynd his frendfchip to fang, with fyne favour.
" It hynderis never for to be heyndly of fpeche.
" He is ane lord riale,
" Has feymly foverane in fale ; · ·
" Ane wourthy wy for to wale.
" Throu all this warld riche.

V.

‘ Thi counfale is convenabill, kynd, and courtefe,
‘ Forthi us likis thi lair, liftin and leir.’
Thai wyis wourthy in weid wend on thair ways;
And caryis to the caftell, cumly and cleir.
Sent ane faynd to the foverane fone, and hym fais,
‘ Thre knichtis fra court cum thay weir.’
Than the ladis belife the lokkis unlaiffis;
On fute frefchly thai frekis foundis but feir.
The renkis raithly can raik into the round hald.
Thair met thame at the entré
Ladys likand to fe,
Thretty knichtis and thre,
That blith war and bald.

VI.

Thai war courtes, and couth, thair knyghthed to kyth:
Athir uthir wele gret, in gretly degré.
Thai bowit to the bernys, that bright war and blith;
Fair in armys to fang, of figuie fa fre.
Syne thay fought to the chalmer fwiftly and fwith,
The gait to the grete lord femely to fe.
And faluft the foverane fone in ane fith,
Courtefly inclinand, and kneland on kne.
Ane blithar wes never borne of bane nor of blude.
All thre in certane
Saluft the foverane,
And he inclynand agane,
Hatles but hude.

VII. Than

VII.

Than Schir Gawyne the gay, gude and graciui,
That ever wes beildit in blis, and bounté embrafit,
Joly, and gentill, and full chevailrus,
That never poynt of his prife wes fundin defafit;
Egir, and ertand, and ryght anterus,
Illuminat with lawte, and with lufe lafit,
Melis of the meſſage to Schir Golagrus,
(Before the riale on raw the renk was noght rafit,)
With ane clene contenance, cumly to knaw;
Said, ' Our foverane Arthour
' Gretis the with honour,
' Has maid us thre as mediatour,
' His meſſage to fchaw.

VIII.

' He is the riallest roy, reverend and rike,
' Of all the rentaris to ryme, or rekin on raw.
' Thare is na leid on life of lordfchip hym like;
' Na nane fa doughty of deid induring his daw.
' Mony burgh, mony bour, mony big bike;
' Mony kynrik to his clame cumly to knaw:
' Maneris full menksfull, with mony deip dike,
' Selcouth war the fevint part to fay at faw.
' Thare anerdis to our nobill to note, quhen hym nedis,
' Tuelf crounit kingis in feir,
' With all thair ſtrang poweir,
' And meny wight weryer
' Worthy in wedis.

G 3   IX. ' It

IX.

' It has bene tauld hym with tong, trow ye full traift,
' Your dedis, your digrité, and your doughtynes;
' Brevit throu bounté for ane of the beft,
' That now is namyt neir of all nobilnes,
' Sa wyde quhare wourfcip walkis be weft ;
' Our feymly foverane hymfelf forfuth will noght cefe
' Quhill he have frely fingit your frendfchip to feft,
' Gif pament, or praier, might mak that purchefe.
' For na largefe my lord, noght will he never let
' Na for na riches to rigne,
' I mak you na lefing;
' It was his maift yarnyng
' Your grant for to get.'

X.

Than faid the fyre of the fail, with fad fembland,
" I thank your gracious grete lord, and his gude will.
" Had never leid of this land, that had been levand,
" Maid ony feuté before, freik, to fulfil,
" I fuld fickirly myfelf be confentand,
" And feik to your foverane, feymly on fyll.
" Sen hail our doughty elderis has bene endurand,]
" Thrivandly in this thede, unchargit as thril,
" If I for obeifance, or boift, to bondage me bynde,
" I war wourthy to be
" Hingit heigh on ane tre,
" That iik creature might fe
" To waif with the wynd.

XI. " Bot

XI.

" Bot favand my fenyeoury fra fubjectioun,
" And my lordfcip unlamyt, withoutin legiance,
" All that I can to yone king, cumly with croun,
" I fall preif all my pane to do hym plefance.
" Baith with body, and beild, bowfum and boun,
" Hym to menfk on mold, withoutin manance.
" Bot nowthir for his fenyeoury, nor for his fummoun,
" Na for dreid of na dede, na for na diftance,
" I will noght bow me ane bak, for berne that is borne.
" Quhill I may my wit wald,
" I think my fredome to hald,
" As my eldaris of ald
" Has done me beforne."

XII.

Thai lufly ledis at that lord thair levis has laught:
Boundit to the bauld king; and boidword hym broght.
Than thai fchupe for to affege fegis unfaught,
Ay the manlyeſt on mold, that maift of myght moght.
Thair wes reſtling and reling but reſt that raught:
Mony fege our the fey to the cité focht:
Schipmen our the ſtreme thai ſtithill full ſtraught,
With alkin wappyns I wys that wes for were wroght.
Thai bend bowis of bras braithly within.
Pellokis paifand to pafe,
Gapand gunnys of brafe,
Grundin ganyeis thair wafe,
That maid ful gret dyn.

G 4   XIII. Thair

XIII.

Thair wes blaving of bemys, braging and beir,
Bretynit doune braid wod maid bewis full bair:
Wrightis welterand doune treis, wit ye but weir,
Ordanit hurdys ful hie in holtis fa haire.
For to greif thair gomys gramest that wer,
To gar the gayest on grund grayne undir geir.
Tbus thai fchupe for ane fall ilk fege feir:
Ilka foveraue his enfenye fhewin has thair.
Ferly fayr wes the feild, flekerit and faw,
With gold and goulis in greyne,
Schynand fcheirly and fcheyne,
The foue, as criftall fa cleyne,
In fcheildis thai fchaw.

XIV.

De it wes mydmorne, and mare, merkit on the day,
Schir GOLAGROS' mery men, menfkful of myght,
In greis, and garatouris, grathit full gay;
Sevyne fcore of fcheildis thai fchew at ane ficht.
Ane helme fet to ilk fcheild, fiker of affay,
With fel laus on loft, lemand full light.
Thus flourit thai the forefront, thair fays to fray,
The frekis, that war fundin ferfe, and forffy in fight.
Ilk knyght his cunyfance kithit full cleir.
Thair names wriften all thare,
Quhat berne that it bare,
That ilk freke quhare he fare,
Might wit quhat he weir.

XV. " Yone

XV.

" Yone is the warlieſt wane," ſaid the wiſe king,
" That ever I wiſt in my walk in all this warld wyde.
" And the ſtraiteſt of ſtuf with richeſe to ring,
" With unabaſit bernys bergane to abide.
" May nane do thame na deir with undoyng,
" Yone houſe is ſa huge hie, fra harme thame to hide.
" Yit ſal I mak thame unruſe, foroutin reſting,
" And reve thame thair rentis with routis full ride,
" Thoght I ſuld fynd thame new notis for this nyne yeir;
" And in his aune preſence
" Heir ſall I make reſidence
" Bot he with forte make defence
" With ſtrenth me to ſteir."

XVI.

" Quhat medis," ſaid SPINAGRUS, " ſic notis to nevin?
" Or ony termis be turnit, I tell you treuly,
" For thair is ſegis in yone ſaill will ſet upone ſevin,
" Or thay be wrangit, I wis, I warne you ilk wy.
" Nane hardiar of hertis undir the hevin :
" Or thay be dantit with dreid erar will thai de.
" And thai with men upone mold be machit full evin,
" Thai ſal be fundin right ferſe, and full of chevalrie.
" Schir, ye ar in your majeſte, your mayne, and your myght,
" Yit within thir dais thre,
" The ſicker ſuth ſall ye ſe,
" Quhat kin men that thai be,
" And how thai dar fight."

XVII. As

XVII.

As the reverend Roy wes reknand upone raw,
With the rout of the round tabill that wes richeft,
The king crounit with gold, cumly to knaw,
With reverend baronis, and beirnes of the beft;
He hard ane bugill blait brym, and ane loud blaw,
As the feynity fone filit to the reft,
Agane gais to ane garet glifnand to fhaw,
Turnit to ane hie toure, that tight wes full treft.
Ane helme of hard fteill in hand has he hynt,
Ane fcheld wroght all of weir,
Semyt wele upone feir;
He grippit to ane greit fpeir,
And furth his wais wynt.

XVIII.

" Quhat fignifyis yone fchene fcheild ?" faid the fenyeour,
" The lufty helme, and the lance, all ar away.
" The brym blaft that he blew, with ane ftevin ftour ?"
Than faid Sir SPYNAGRUS with fpeche, "The futh fall I fay.
" Yone is ane freik in his forte, and frefch in his flour,
" To fe that his fchire weid be ficker of affay
" He thinkis provefe to preve, for his paramour,
" And prik in your prefence to purchefe his pray.
" Forthi makis furth ane man, to mach him in feild;
" That knawin is for cruel,
" Doughty dyntis to dell
" That for the maiftry mell
" With fchaft and with fcheild."

XIX. Than

.XIX.

Than wes the king wordir glaid, and callit GAUDIFEIR;
Quhilum in *Britane* that berne had baronyis braid.
And he gudly furth gais, and graithit his geir;
And bufkit him to battel, without mair abaid.
That wy walit, I wis, all wedis of weir,
That nedit hym to note gif 'he nane'had.
Bery broune wes the blonk, burely and braid,
Upone the mold quhare thai met, before the myd day.
With lufly lancis, and lang,
Ane feire feild can thai fang,
On ftedis ftalwart and ftrang,
Baith blanchart and bay.

XX.

GAUDIFEIR, and GALIOT, in glemand fteil wedis,
As glavis glowand on gleid, grymly thai ride.
Wondir fternly thai fteir on thair ftent ftedis;
Athir berne fra his blonk borne wes that tide.
Thai rufchit up rudly, quha fa right redis;
Out with fuerdis thai fwang, fra thair fchalk fide.
Thairwith wraithly thai wirk, thai wourthy in wedis,
Hewit on the hard fteil, and hurt thame in the hide.
Sa wondir frefchly thai trekis frufchit in feir,
Throw all the harnes thai hade,
Baith birny and breift plade,
Thairin wappynis couth wade,
Wis ye but weir.

XXI. Thus

.XXI.

Thus thai faught upone fold, with ane fel fair,
Quhill athir berne in that breth bokit in blude.
Thus thai mellit on mold, ane myle way and mair,
Wraithly wrobt as thei war, witlefe and wode.
Baith thai fegis forfuth, fadly and fair,
Thoght thai war aftonait, in the ftou: ftithly thai ftude.
The feght fa felly thai fang, with ane frefch fair,
Quhill GAUDIFEIR, and GALIOT, baith to grund yhude.
GAUDIFEIR gat up agane, throu Goddis grete mightis.
Abone him wichtely he wan,
With the craft that he can.
Thai lovit God, and Sanct An,
The king and his knightis.

XXII.

Than wes GALIOT the gome hynt·intill ane hald.
GOLAGRUS grew in greif grymly in hart;
And callit Schir RIGAL of *Rone*, ane renk that wes bald,
" Quhill this querrell be quyt I cover never in quert.
" With wailit wapnis of were, even on yone wald,
" On ane fterand fteid, that fternly will ftert,
" I pray the, for my faik, that it be deir fald ;
" Was never fa unfound fet to my hert."
That gome gudly furth gays, and graithit his gere ;
Blew ane blaft of ane horne,
As wes the maner beforne ;
Scheld and helm has he borne
Away with his fpere.

XXIII. The

XXIII.

The king crounit with gold this cumpas wel knew,
And callit Schir RAUNALD, cruell and kene;
‘ Gif ony preſſis to this place, for proues to perſew,
‘ Schaip thé evin to the ſchalk in thi ſchroud ſchene.’
The deir dight him to the deid be the day dew,
His birny, and his baſnet, burniſt full bene ;
Baith his horſe, and his geir, wes of ane hale hew,
With gold and goulis ſa gay, graithit in grene.
Ane ſchene ſcheild, and ane ſchaft that ſcharply was ſched ;
Thre berhedis he bair,
As his eldaris did air,
Quhilk beirnis in *Britane* wair
Of his blude bled.

XXIV.

Quhen the day can daw deirly on hight,
And the ſone in the ſky wes ſchynyng ſo ſchir,
Fra the caſtell thair come cariand ane knight,
Cloſit in clene ſteill, upone ane courſyr.
Schir RANNALD to his riche ſteid raikit full riht,
Lighly lap he on loft, that luſly of lyre ;
Athir laught has thair lance, that lemyt ſo light.
On twa ſtedis thai ſtraid, with ane ſterne ſchiere.
Togiddir freſchly thai frekis fruſchit in ſay.
Thair ſperis in ſplendris ſprent,
On ſcheldis ſchenkit and ſcheut,
Evin our thair hedis went
In feild fir away.

XXV. Thai

XXV.

Thai lufty ledis belife lightit on the land,
And laught oot fwerdis lufly and langt
Thair ftedis ftakkerit in the ftour, and ftude ftammerand;
Al to ftiffillit; and ftonayt; the ftrak is war fa ftrang;
Athir berne braithly ber, with ane bright brand;
On fute frefchly thai frekis feightin thai fang;
Thai hewit on hard fteil hartly with hand,
Qubil the fpalis, and the fparkis, fpedely out fprang.
Schir R A N N A L D raught to the renk ane rout wes unryde;
Clenely in the collair;
Fifty mailyeis and mair,
Evin of the fchuldir he fchair
Ane wound that wes wyde.

XXVI.

Thus thai faucht on fute, on the fair feild;
The blude famyt thame fra on feild quhare thai found;
All the bernys on the bent, about that beheild,
For pure forow of that fight thai fighit unfound;
Schire teris fchot fra fchalkis fchene under fcheild,
Quhen thai foundrit ane fel fey to the grund.
Baith thair hartis can brift braithly but beild:
Thair wes na ftalvart unftonait, fo fterne was the ftound.
Schir R A N N A L D I S body wes broght to the bright tent.
Syne to the caftel of ftone
Thai had Schir R I O A L of *Rone*;
With mekil murnyng and mone
Away with him went.

PART III.

P A R T   III.

A R G U M E N T.

RIGAL and RANALD buried: GOLOGRAS fends four
knights, I.—Four oppofe them, II.—The combat and
its iffuc, III, IV, V, VI, VII.—O-her knights fight,
VIII, IX.—GOLOGRAS refolves to fight himfelf, X.
—SPINAGROS advifes ARTHUR to appoint a champion, who names GAWAN, XI, XII.—Advice of
SPINAGROS to GAWAN, XIII, XIV.—KAY rides out.
and fights a knight, XV, XVI.—The knight yields,
and KAY leads him to ARTHUR, XVII, XVIII.—
GOLOGRAS and GAWAN appear, XIX, XX.—The
combat defcribed at great length, XXI, XXII, XXIII,
XXIV, XXV, XXVI, XXVII.

I.

Thus endit the avynantis with mekil honour:
Yit has men thame in mynd for thair manhede.
Thair bodeis wes beryit, baith in ane hour:
Set fegis for thair faullis, to fyng and to reid.
Than GOLOGRUS graithit of his men in glifnand armour,
Ane Schir LOWIS the lele, ane lord of that leid;
Ane uthir heght EDMOND, that provit paramour;
The thrid heght Schir BANTELLAS, the batal to leid;
The ferd wes ane weryour, worthy and wight,
His name wes Schir SANGUEL,
Cumly and cruel.
Thir four, treuly to tell,
Foundis to the fight.

II. Schir

II.

Schir LYONEL to Schir LOUYS wes levit with ane lance:
Schir EWIN to Schir EDMOND athir full evin:
Schir BEDWAR to Schir BANTELLAS, to enschew his chance,
That baith war nemmyt in neid nobil to nevin: ~
To Schir SANGWEL soght gude GYROMALANCE.
Thus thai mellit, and met with ane stout stevin.
Thir lusty ledis on the land, without legiance,
With seymely scheidis to schew thai set upone sevin:
Thir cumly kinghtis to kyth ane cruel courfe maid.
The frekis felloune in feir
Wondir stoutly can steir,
With geir grundin full cleir
Rudly thai raid.

III.

Than thair hors with thair hochis sic harmis couth hint,
As trasit in unquart quakand thai stand.
The frekis freschly thai sure, as fyre out of flynt,
Thair lufly lances thai loissit, and lichtit on the land.
Right styth stuffit in steill thai stotit na stynt;
Bot bufkit to battaile, with birny and brand.
Thair riche birnys thai bet dersly with dynt;
Hewis down in grete haist hartly with hand.
Thai migh·y men upon mold ane riale courfe maid;
Quhill clowis of clene maill
Hoppit out as the haill:
Thay beirnys in the bataill
Sa bauldly thai baid.

IV. Thai

IV.

Thai bet on fa bryimly, thai beirnys on the bent;
Briſtis birneis with brandis burniſt full bene :
Throu thair fchene fcheildis thair fchuldris var fchent ;
Fra fchalkis fchot fchire blude our fcheildis fo fchene;
Ryngis of rank ſteill rattillit and rent :
Gomys grifly on the grund, grains on the grene;
The Roy ramyt for reuth, richeſt of rent,
For thair of his knightis, cruel and kene.
Sa wondir frefchly thair force thai freſt on the feildis ;
So huge wes the mellé,
Wes nane fa couth fe
Quhilk gome fuld govern the gre,
Bot God that all weildis.

V.

The Wyis wroght uther grete wandrëth, and weuch;
Wirkand woundis full wyde, with wapnis of were;
Helmys of hard ſteill thai hatterit and heuch.
In that hailfing thai hynt grete harmys and here;
All to turnit thair intyre traiſtly and tewch ;
Burniſt bladis of ſteill throw birneis thay bore;
Schort fverdis of fcheith fmertly thay dreuch.
Athir freik to his fallow, with fellonne affere;
Throw platis of poliſt ſteil thair poyntis can pafe.
All thus thai threw in that thrang
Stalvert ſtraks, and ſtrang:
With daggaris derfly thay dang
Thai doughtyis on dafe.

VI.

Schir LYONELL Schir LOWES laught has in hand ;
And fefit is SANGWELL with GIROMALANS the gude ;
Schir EVIN has Schir EDMOND laid on the land,
Braithly bartynit with baill, bullerand in blude.
Schir BEDWAR to Schir BANTELLAS yaldis up his brand.
In that ftalwart ftour, thay ftyth men in ftude,
Wes nane forffy on fold, that wes feghtand,
Unmanglit and marrit, myghtles in mude.
Wes nane fa proud of his part that prifit quhen he yeid,
BEDWER and LYONELL
War led to the Caftell,
The cumly knight SANGWELL
To ARTHOUR thay led.

VII.

Schir EDMOND loiffit has his life, and laid is full law :
Schir EVIN hurtis has hynt hidwife, and fair ;
Knightis caryis to the corfe was cumly to knaw,
And had hym to the Caftell, with mekill hard cair.
Thai did to that doughty as the dede aw.
Uthir four of the folk foundis to the fair,
That wes dight to the dede, be the day can daw.
Than faid bernys bald, brym as bair,
' We fal evin that is od, or end in the pane.'
Thai ftuffit helmys in hy,
Breift plait, and birny,
Thay renkis maid reddy
All geir that myght gane.

VIII. Schir

VIII.

Schir AGALUS, Schir EWMOND, honeſt and habill;
Schir MYCHIN, Schir MELIGOR, men of grete eſtait;
Than ſtertis out ane ſterne Knyght, ſtalwart and ſtabill,
Ane berne that hight Schir HEW, hardy and hait.
Nou will I rekkin the renkis of the round tabill,
That has traiſtly thame tight to governe that gait.
Furth faris the folk, but fenyeing or fabill,
That bemyt war be the lord, luffsum of lait.
Schir CADOR of *Cornwell*, cumly and cleir;
Schir OWALES, Schir IWELL,
Schir MYREOT mighty in mell;
Thir four, trewly to tell,
Foundis n feir.

IX.

Thair wes na trety of treux, trow ye full traiſt,
Quhen thai myghty can mach, on mold quhair thai met.
Thai brochit blonkis to thair fydis out of blude braiſt:
Thair lufly lancis thai loiſſit, and lightit but let.
Sadillis thai temyt tyt, thir trew men and traiſt;
Braidit out brandis on birnys thai bet:
As fyre that fleis fra the flynt, thay fochtin ſa faſt,
With vengeand wapnis of were throw wedis thai wet.
It war teirfull to tell treuly the tend
Of thair ſtrife ſa ſtrang.
The feght ſo fellely thai fang
Thoght it leſtit never ſo lang
Yit laught it ane end.

　　　　　　X. Schir

X.

Schir OVILES, Schir IWELL, in handis war hynt,
And to the lufly caftell war led in ane lyng.
Thairwith the ftalwartis in ftour can ftolin and ftynt:
And baith Schir AGALUS ard Schir HEW was led to the
    Kyng.
Than Schir GOLOGRASE, for greif his gray ene brynt,
Wod wraith ; and the wynd his handis can wryng.
Yit makis he mery magry, quhafa mynt:
Said " I fal bargane abyde, and ane end bryng.
" To morne fickirly myfelf fall feik to the feild."
He bufkit to ane barfray,
Twa fmal bellis rang thay.
Than feymly ARTHUR can fay,
Wes fchune undir fcheild.

XI.

" Quhat fignifyis yon rynging ?" faid the ryale.
Than faid SPYNAGROS with fpeche, ' Schir *fens peir*
' That fall I teli yow with tong trewly in taill.
' The wy that weildis yone wane, I warn you but weir,
' He thinkis his aune felf fhall do for his dail.
' Is nane fa provit in this part of pyth is his peir.
' You worthis, wifly to wirk, ane wy for to wail,
' That fal duchtely his deid do with yone deir.
' He is the forfieft freik, be fortoune his freynd,
' That I wait levand this day.'
Than Schir GAWINE the gay
Prayt for the journay
That he might furth wend,

XII. Th

XII.

The kiug grantit the gait to Schir GAWANE.
And prayt to the grete God to grant him his grace,
Him to fave and to falf that is our foverane,
As he is maker of man, and alkyn myght haife.
Than Schir SPINAGROS the freik was ferly unfane;
Murnyt for Schir GAWYNE, and mekil mayne maife.
And faid, " for his faik that faiklefe wes flane,
" Tak nocht yone keyn knight to countir in this hard cais.
" Is nane fi ftalwarr, in ftour with ftoutnis to ftand,
" Of all that langis to the king.
" The mair is my murnyng,
" Ye fuld this fell fechting
" Hynt upone hand.

XIII.

" Sen ye are fa wourfchipfull, and wourthy in were,
" Demyt with the derreft maift doughty in deid,
" Yone berne in the battale will ye noght forbere
" For all the mobil on the mold merkit to meid."
' Gif I de doughtely, the les is my dere.
' Thoght he war SAMPSONE himfelf, fa me Crifte reid,
' I forfaik noght to fight, for al his grete feir,
' I do the weill for to wit, doutlefe but dreid.'
Than faid Schir SPYNAGROSE, " Sen ye will of neid
" Be boun to the battale,
" Wirkis with counfale,
" It fall right gret avale,
" And do it in dede.·

H 3   XIV. " Quhen

XIV.

" Quhen ye mach hym on mold, merk to hym evin ;
" And bere ye your bright lance in myddis his fcheild,
" Mak that courfe cruel, fos Cryftis lufe of hevin ;
" And fyne wiike as I wife your wappins to weild.
" Be he ftonayt yone fterne, ftout beis his ftevin,
" He wourdis brym as ane bair, that bydis na beild.
" Noy you noght at his note, that nobill is to nevin,
" Suppofe his dyntis be deip dentit in your fcheild.
" Tak na haift upone hand quhat happunys may hynt,
" Bot lat the riche man rage,
" And fecht in his curage,
" To fwyng with fuerd, quhil he fuage ;
" Syne dele ye your dynt.

XV.

" Quhen he is ftuffit, thair ftrike, and hald hym on fteir,
" Sa fall ye ftonay yone flowt, fuppofe he be ftrang.
" Thus may ye lippin on the lake throu lair that I leir ;
" But gif ye wirk as wife you worthis that wrang."
The king, and his knichtis, cumly and cleir,
In armour dewly hym dight, be the day fprang,
Than wes Schir KAY wondir wo, wit ye but weir,
In defalt of ane freik the fighting to fang.
That gome gudely furth gais, and graithit his geir,
Ivin to the caftell he raid,
Hewit in ane dern flaid ;
Sa come ane knight as he baid,
Anairmit of weir.

XVI. That

XVI.

That knight bufkit to Schir KAY, on ane fteid broune,
Braiffit in birneis, and bafnet full bene.
He cryis his enfenye, and conteris hym full foune;
And maid ane courfe curagioufe, cruell and kene.
Thair lufly lancis thai loiffit, and lightit baith doune,
And girdit out fuerdis on the grund grene;
And hewit on hard fteill, hartlie but houne;
Rude reknyng raife thair renkis betuene.
Thair mailyeis with melle thay merkit in the medis,
The blude of thair bodeis
Throw breift plait, and birneis,
As roife ragit on rife,
Our ran thair riche wedis.

XVII.

Thus thai faught upone fute, without fenyeing,
The fparkis flaw in the feild, as fyre out of flynt.
Thai lufly ledis in lyke thai layid on in ane ling:
Delis thair full doughtely mony derf dynt.
Dufchand on deir wedis dourty thai dyng:
Hidwife hurtis, and huge, haiftely thai hynt.
That knight carpit to Schir KAY of difcomforting,
' Of this ftonay, and ftour, I rede that ye ftynt.
' I will yeild the my brand, fen na better may bene.
' Quhair that fortoune will faill
' Thair may na befynes availl.'
He braidit up his ventaill
That clofit wes clene.

XVIII.

For to reſſave the brand the berne wes full blith ;
For he wes byrſit, and befr, and braithly bledand.
Thoght he wes myghtles, his mercy can he thair myth,
And wald that he nane harme hynt, with hart and with hand,
Thai caryit baith to the kynde cumly to kyth.
Thair lancis war loiſſit, and left on the land.
Than ſaid he loud upone loft, " Lord will ye lyth,
" Ye ſal nane torfeir betyde, I tak upone hand.
" Na myſliking have in hart, nor have ye na dout,
" Oft in Romans I reid
" Airly ſporne luit ſpeid."
The king to the pailyeoun gart lcid
The knight that wes ſtout.

XIX.

Thai hynt of his harueſe, to helyn his wound :
Lechis war noght to lait with ſawis ſa ſle.
With that meny fieſch freik can to the feild found,
With GOLOGRAS in his geir grete of degre.
Armyt in rede gold, and rubeis ſa round,
With mony riche relikis, riale to ſe.
Thair wes on GOLOGRAS, quhair he glaid on the ground,
Frenyeis cf fyne ſilk fratit full fre.
Apone ſterand ſtedis, trappit to the hell,
Sexty ſchalkis full ſchene,
Cled in armour ſa clene ;
No wy wantit, I wene ;
All ſtuffit in ſteill.

XX. That

XX.

That berne rajd on ane boulk, of ane ble quhite,
Blyndit all with bright gold, and beriallis bright,
'Io tell of his deir weid war doutles delite,
And alfe ter for to tell the travallis war tight.
His name and his nobillay wes noght for to nyte:
Thair wes na hathill fa heich, be half ane foie hicht.
He lanfit out our ane land, and drew noght ane lyte;
Quhair he fuld fraflyn his force and fangin his fight.
Be that Schir GAWYNE the gay wes graithit in his gere,
Cummyng on the ta fyde,
Hovand battale to abyde,
All reddy famyne to ryde,
With fcheld a.d with fpere.

XXI.

Thir lufly ledis on the land, left be thame allane,
'I uke no uthir, fremyt, nor freyndis, bot found tham fra.
Twa rynnyng renkis raith the riolyfe has tane;
I k fieik to his feir to freftin his fa.
'I hai gird one tua grete horfe, on grund quhil thai grane;
The trew helmys, and traift, in tathis thai ta.
The rochis reirdit with the rafch, quhen thai famyne ran:
Thair fperis in the feild in flendris gart ga.
The ftedis flakerit in the ftour, for ftreking on ftray.
The bernys bowit abak,
Sa woundir rude wes the rak:
Quhilk that happynnit the lak
Couth na leid fay.

XX. Thai

XXII.

Thai brayd fra thair blonkis befely and bane,
Syne laught out foerdis lang and lufly.
And hewit on hard fteill wondir hawtane:
Baith war thai haldin of hartis heynd and hardy,
GOLOGRAS grew in greif at Schir GAWANE:
On the hight of the hard fteill he hyt hym in hy;
Pertly put with his pith at his pefane,
And fulyeit of the fyne maill may than fyfty.
The knight ftaterit with the ftraik, all ftonayt in ftouad;
Sa woundir fcharply he fchair,
The berne that the brand bair,
Schir GAWYNE, with ane fell fair,
Can to his faa found.

XXIII.

With ane bitand brand, burly and braid,
Quhilk oft in battale had bene his bute, and his belde,
He leit gird to the grome, with greif that he had,
And claif throw the cantell of the clene fchelde.
Throw birny, and breift-plait, and bordour, it baid;
The fulye of the fyne gold fell in the feild.
The rede blude with the rout folowit the blaid,
(For all the wedis, I wife, that the wy weild,)
Throw clafpis of clene gold, and clowis fa cleir,
Thair with Schir GOLOGRAS the fyre,
In mekil anger and ire,
Alfe ferfe as the fyre,
Leit fle to his feir,

XXIV. Sic

XXIV.

Sic dintis he delt to that doughty,
Leit hym deftanyt to danger and dreid.
Thus wes he handillit full hait, that hawtane in hy;
The fcheld in countir he keft our his cleir weid;
Hewit on hard fteill woundir haiftely;
Gart beryallis hop of the hathill about hym on breid,
Than the king unto Crifte keft up ane cry;
Said, "Lord, as thow life lent to levand in leid,
" As thow formit all frute to fofter our fude,
" Grant me comfort this day,
" As thou art God verray."
Thus prais the king, in affray,
For GAWYNE the gude.

XXV.

GOLOGRAS at GAWYNE in fic ane greif grew,
As lyoune for falt of fude faught on the fold;
With baith his handis in haift that haltane couth hew,
Gart flanys hop of the hathill that haltane war hold.
Birny, and breift-plait, bright for to fchew,
Mony mailye, and plait, war marrit on the mold.
Knichtis ramyt for reuth, Schir GAWYNE thai rew,
That doughty delit with hym fa, for dout he war defold,
Sa wondir fcharply he fchare, throu his fchene fchroud:
His fcheild he chopit hym fra,
In twenty pecis, and ma.
Schir WAWANE writhit for wa
Witlefe and woud.

XXVI. Thus

XXVI.

Thus wourthit Schir GAWYEE wraith and wepand,
And ftraik to that ftern knight, but ony ftynt:
All epgrevit the grome, with ane bright brand;
And delt thairwith doughtely meny derf dynt.
Throw byrny, and breift-plait, bordour, and band,
He leit fle to the freke, as fyre out of flynt.
He hewit on with grete haift, hartly with hand;
Hakkit throw the hard weid to the hide hynt,
Throw the ftuf with the ftraik, ftapalis and ftanis.
Schir WAWINE, wourthy in wail,
Half ane fpan at ane fpail,
Quhare his harnes wes hail,
He hewit attanis.

XXVII.

Thus raithly the riche berne raffit his array.
The tothir ftertis ane bak, the fterne that wes ftout,
Hit Schir GAWAYNE on the gere, quhill grevit wes the
    gay,
Betit doune the bright gold, and beryallis about;
Scheddit his fchire wedis fcharply away;
That lufly lappit war on loft, he gar thame law lout.
The fterne ftakrit with the ftraik, and ftertis on ftray,
Quhill neir his refoune wes tynt; fa rude wes the rout,
The beryall's on the land of bratheris gart light;
Rubeis and fapheir;
Precious ftanis that weir;
Thus drefe thai wedis fa deir,
That dantely wes dight.

PART

P A R T IV.

A R G U M E N T.

The combat between GAWAN and GOLOGRAS conti-
nues, and GOLOGRAS has a fall, I. II.—GAWAN infifts on his yielding : he refufes, III. IV.—The lords
and ladies of the caftle pray for GOLOGRAS, V.—
GAWAN again perfuades him to yield, but he refufes,
VI. VII.—GOLOGRAS propofes to GAWAN to attend
him to the caftle, VIII.—GAWAN affents and
attends him, IX. X.—Grief of ARTHUR'S people,
who think GAWAN vanquifhed, XI.—GOLOGRAS en-
tertains GAWAN, XII.—GOLOGRAS confults his peers,
if they would have him reign when conquered, or lofe
his life? They anfwer, that he fhall live and reign,
XIII. XIV. XV.—GOLOGRAS offers homage, and de-
claims on fortune, XVI. XVII. XVIII. XIX.—GOLO-
GRAS and his court go to ARTHUR, XX.—Who fuf-
pects they come in war, but SPINAGROS fays not,
and ARTHUR receives them kindly, XXI. XXII.—
GOLOGRAS makes a fpeech and homage to ARTHUR,
XXIII. XXIV. XXV.—ARTHUR goes to the caftle, and
feafts and hunts by the Rhone for nine days, XXVI.
XXVII.—ARTHUR declares GOLOGRAS free, XXVIII.

I. Thai

I.

Thai gyrd on fa grymly, in ane grit ire,
Baith Schir GAVINE the grome, and GOLOGRAS the
    knight.
The fparkis flew in the feild, as fagottis of fire,
Sa wundir frely thai frekis fangis the fight.
Thai lufchit, and laid on, thai luflyis of lyre.
King ARTHUR Ihefu befoght, feymly with fight,
" As thou art foverane God, fickerly, and fyre,
" At thow wald warys fra wo WAVANE the wight !
" And grant the frekis en fold farar to fall.
Baith thair honouris to faif,
At Crift with credence thai craif,
Knight, fquyar, and knaif;
And thus pray thay all.

II.

Thai mellit on with malice, thay myghtyis in mude;
Mankit throu mailyeis and maid thame to mer :
Wraithly wroght, as thai war witlefe and wod.
Be that Schir WAWANE, the wy, likit the wer :
The ble of his bright weid wes bulerand in blude;
Thairwith the nobill in neid nyghit hym ner,
Straik hym with ane fteill brand, in ftede quhare he ftude,
The fchild in fardillis can fle in feild, away fer.
The tothir hyt hym agane, with ane hard fuerd,
As he loutit our ane bra,
His feit founderit hym fra.
Schir GOLOGRAS graithly can ga
Grulingis to erd.

III. Of

III.

Or ever he gat up agane gude Schir GAWANE
Grippit to Schir GOLOGRAS, on the grand grene.
Thair of gromys wes glaid, gudly, and gane,
Lovit Crifte of that cafe, with hartis fa clene.
Ane daggar dayntely dight that dowghty has drawne,
Than he carpit to the knight, cruel and kene;
" Gif thow luffis thi life lelely noght to layne,
" Yeld me thi bright brand, burnift fa bene.
" I rede thow wirk as I wife; or war the betide."
The tothir anfuerit fchortly,
' Me thinks farar to dee,
' Than fchamyt be verralie
' Ane fclander to byde.

IV.

' Wes I never yit defoullit, nor fylit in fame;
' Nor nane of my eldaris, that ever I hard nevin:
' Bot ilk berne has bene unbundin with blame,
' Ringand in rialté, and reullit thame felf evin.
' Sall never fege wndir fon fe me with fchame,
' Na luke on my lekame, with light, nor with levin:
' Na nane of the nynt degre have noy of my name;
' I fwere be futhfaft God, that fettis all on fevin.
' Bot gif that wourfchip of were win me away,
' I trete for na favour.
' Do furth thy devoir.
' Of me gettis thou na more,
' Doutles this day.'

7   V. Lordingis

V.

Lordingis and ladyis, in the caſtell on loft,
Quhen thai faw thair liege lord laid on the landis,
Mony ſweit thing of ſware ſwownit full oft;
Wyis wourthit for wo to wringin thair handis.
Wes nowther ſolace, nor ſang, thair ſorrow to ſoft:
Ane ſayr ſtonay, and ſtour, at thair hartis ſtandis.
On Criſte cumly thai cry, " On croce as thou coft,
" With thi bliſſit blude to bring us out of bandis,
" Lat never our ſoverane his cauſe with ſchame to encheiſ!
" Mary, fareſt of face,
" Beſeik thi ſone in this cace,
" Ane drop of his grete grace
" He grant us to geif."

VI.

Thus the ledis on loft in langour war lent.
The lordis, on the tothir ſide, for liking thay leugh.
Schir GAWYNE tretit the knight to turn his entent,
For he wes wondar wa to wirk hym mare wugh.
" Schir ſay for thi ſelf, thow ſeis thow art ſchent,
" It may nocht mend the ane myte to mak it ſa teugh.
" Riſe and raik to our Roy, richeſt of rent,
" Thow ſal be newit at neid with nobillay eneuch;
" And dukit in our duchery all the duelling."
' Than war I woundir unwis
' To purcheſe proffit for priſe,
' Quhare ſchame ay overlyis
' All my lcving.

VII. The

VII.

' The fege that 'fchrenks for na fchame, the fchent might
    hym fchend,
' That mare luffis his life, than lois upone erd.
' Sal never freik on fold, fremmyt nor freynd,
' Gar me lurk for ane luke, lawit nor lerd.
' For quhafa with wourfchip fall of this warld wende
' Thair will nane wyis, that ar wis, wary the werd.
' For ony trety may tyd, I tell thé the teynd,
' I will noght turn myn entent, for all this warld brerd:
' Or I pair of pris ane penny worth in this place,
' For befandis, or beryell.
' I knaw my aune quarrell.
' I dreid not the perill,
' To dee in this cace.'

VIII.

Schir GAWYNE rewit the renk, that wes riale;
And faid to the reverend, riche, and rightuis,
" How may I fuccour the found, femely in fale,
" Before this pepill in plane, and pair noght thy pris?"
' That fall I tel the with tong, trewly in tale.
' Wald yow denye the in deid to do my devis,
' Lat it worth, at my wil, the wourfchip to wale,
' As I had wonnyn thé of were, wourthy and wis.
' Syne cary to the caftel, quhare I have maift cure.
' Thus may you faif me fra fyte.
' As I am criftynit perfite,
' I fall thi yndnes quyte,
' And fauf thyn honoure.'

IX.

" That war hard," faid the heynd, " fa have I gude hele!
" Ane woundir peralous poynt, partenyng grete plight,
" To foner in thi gentrice, but fignete or fele,
" And I before faw the never fickerly with fight.
" To leif in thi lauté, and thow war unlele,
" Than had I caffin in cair mony kene knight.
" Bot I knaw thow art kene, and alfe cruell,
" Or thow be fulyeit fey freke in the fight,
" I do me in thi gentrice, be drightin fa deir."
He lenyit up in the place.
The tothir raithly upraife.
Gat never grome fic ane grace
In feild of his feir.

X.

Than thei nobillis at neid yeid to thair note new ;
Frefchly foundis to feght all fenye, and thair fair.
Tua fchort fuerdis of fcheith fmertly thai drew,
Than thai mellit on mold ane myl wan, and mare.
Wes nawthir Cafar, nor King, thair quentance that knew ;
It femyt be thair contenance that kendillit wes care.
Syne thai traift in the feild, throw trety of trew ;
Put up thair brandis fa braid, burly and bair.
GOLOGRAS, and GAWYNE, gracious and gude,
Yeid to the caftell of ftane,
As he war yoldin and tane.
The king precious in ane
Sair murnand in mude.

XI.

The Roy ramand full raith, that reuth wes to fe,
And raikit full redles to his riche tent.
The watter wet his chekis, that fchalkis myght fe,
As all his welthis in warld had bene away went.
And othir bernys, for barrat, blakynnit thair ble :
Braithly bundin in baill, thair breiftis war blent.
"The flour of knighthede is caught throu his cruelté !
" Now is the Round Tabil rebutit, richeft of rent !
" Quhen wourfchipfull WAWANE, the wit of our were,
" Is led to ane prefonne,
" Now failyeis gude fortoune !"
The King, cumly with croune,
Grat mony falt tere.

XII.

Quhen that GAWYNE, the gay, grete of degré,
Wes cummyn to the caftel, cumly and cleir,
Gromys of that garifoune maid gamyn and gle ;
And ledis lofit thair lord, lufly of lyere.
Beirdis beildit in blife, brighteft of ble.
The tothir knightis maid care of ARTHURIS here.
All thus with murnyng, and myrth, thai maid mellé,
Ay quhil the fegis were fet to the fuppere.
The feymly foverane of the fail marfchel he wes.
He gart Schir GAWYNE upga.
His wife, his doghter alfua ;
And of that mighty na ma,
War fet at the des.

I 2

XIII.

He gart at ane feteburd the ftrangearis begin;
The maift feymly in fale ordanit thame fete,
Ilk knyght ane cumly lady that cleir wes of kyn;
With kynde contenance the renk couth thame rehete.
Quhen thai war machit at mete, the mare and the myn,
And ay the meryeft on mold marfchalit at mete,
Than faid he lowd upone loft, the lord of that in,
To al the beirnys about, of gre that wes grete;
" Lufly ledis in land lythis me til!"
He ftraik the burd with ane wand,
The quhilk he held in hand.
Thair wes na word muvand,
Sa war thair all ftil.

XIV.

" Heir ye ar gaderit in groffe, at the greteft,
" Of gomys that grip has undir my godvernyng;
" Of baronis, and burowis, of braid land the beft,
" And alfe the meryeft on mold has intrometting.
" Cumly knightis in this cace I mak you requeft,
" Freyndfully, but falfet, or ony fenyeing,
" That ye wald to me treuly, and traift,
" Tell your entent, as tuiching this thing,
" That now hingis on my hart; fa have I gude hele,
" It tuichis myne honour fa neir,
" Ye mak me plane anfueir;
" Thairof I you requeir,
" I may noght concele.

XV. " Say

XV.

" Say me ane chois, the tane of thir twa,
" Quhethir ye like me lord, laught in the feild ;
" Or ellis my life at the left lelely forga,
" And boune you to fum berne that myght be your beild."
The wourthy wyis, at that word, wox woundir wa.
Than thai wift thair foverane wes fchent undir fcheild.
' We wil na favour here fenye, to frende, nor to fa ;
' We like yow ay, as our lord, to were, and to weild.
' Your lordfchip we may noght forga, alfe lang as we leif.
' Ye fal be our governour,
' Quhil your dais may endure,
' In eife and honour ;
' For chance that may cheif.'

XVI.

Quhen thai avenand, and honeft, had maid this anfwer,
And had tald thair entent trewly him till ;
Than Schir GOLOGRAS the gay, in gudly maneir,
Said to thai fegis, femely on fyll,
How wourfchipful WAVANE had wonnin him on weir,
To wirk him wandreth, or wough, quhilk war his wil ;
How fair him fell in feght ; fyne how he couth forbere ;
In fight of his foverane, this did the gentill.
" He has me favit fra fyte, throw his gentrice.
" It war fyn, but recure,
" The knightis honour fuld fmure,
" That did me this honoure,
" Quhilk maift is of price.

I 3   XVII. " I

XVII.

" I aught, as prynce, him to prifc, for his prouefe,
" That wanyt noght my wourfchip, as he that al wan,
" And at his bidding full bane, blith to obeife,
" 'J his berne full of bewté, that all my baill blan ;
" 1 mak that knawin, and kend, his grete kyndnes,
" The countirpas to kyth to him gif I can."
He raikit to Schir GAWINE, right in ane race ;
Said, "Schir, I knaw, be conqueft, thou art ane kynd man,
" Quhen my life, and my dede, wes baith at thi will,
" Thy frendfchip frely I fand.
" Now wil I be obeyand ;
" And mak the manrent with hand,
" As right is, and fkill.

XVIII.

" Sen fortoune cachis the cours, throu hir quentys,
" I did it noght for nane dreid that I had to de ;
" Na for na fauting of hart, na for na fantife,
" Quhare Crifte cachis the cours, it rynnys quently.
" May nowther power, nor pith, put him to prife
" Quhan on fortone quhelmys the quheil, thair gais grace by.
" Quha may his danger endure, or deftanye defpife,
" That led men in langour, ay leftand in ly ?
" The date na langar may endure, na drightin devinis,
" Ilk man may kyth, be his cure,
" Baith knight, king, and Empriour ;
" And mufe in his myrour,
" And mater maift mineis.

XIX. HECTOUR,

XIX.

" Hectour, and Alexander, and Julius Cesar;
" David, and Josue, and Judas the gent;
" Sampsone, and Salamon that wife and wourthy war,
" And that ryngis on erd, richeft of rent;
" Quhen thai met at the merk, than might thai na mair;
" To fpeid thame our the fpere feild eufpringing thai fprent.
" Quhen fortune worthis unfrende, than failieis welefair;
" Thair ma na trefour ourtak, nor twyn his entent.
" All erdly riches, and rufe, is nought in thair garde.
" Quhat menis fortoune be fkill,
" Ane gude chance, or ane ill;
" Ilkane be werk, and he will,
" Is wourthy his rewarde.

XX.

" Schir Hallolkis, Schir Hewis, heynd and hardy;
" Schir Lyonel lufly, and alfe Schir Bedwere;
" Schir Wawane the wife knight, wicht and wourthy,
" Carys furth to the king, cumly and clere.
" Alfe myfelf fall pafe with yow reddy;
" My kyth, and my caftel, compt his conquere."
Thai war arait full raith, that ryale cumpany,
Of lordis, and ladis lufsum to lere;
With grete lightis on loft, that gave grete leime;
Sexty torcheis ful bright,
Before Schir Gologras the knyght.
That wes ane femely fyght,
In ony riche reime.

XXI.

All efrayt of that fair wes the frefch king,
Wend the wyis had bene wroght all for the weir;
Lordis laught thair lancis, and went in ane lyng;
And graithit thame to the gait in thair greif geir.
SPYNOK fpekis with fpeche, faid, " move you na thing,
" It femys faughtnyng thai feik, Ife be thair feir.
" Yone riche cumis arait in riche robbing:
" I trow this devore be done; I dout for na deir.
" I wait Schir GAWANE the gay has graithit his gait,
" Betwix Schir GOLOGRAS, and he,
" Gude contenance I fe:
" And uthir knightis fo fre
" Lufsum of lait."

XXII.

The renk raikit to the Roy, with his riche rout;
Sexty fchalkis that fchene, feymly to fchaw,
Of banrenttis, and baronis, bauld hym about,
In clathis of cleyne gold, cumly to knaw.
To the lordly on loft that lufly can lour,
Before the riale renkis, richeft on raw;
Saluft the bauld berne, with ane blith wout,
Ane furlenth before his folk, on feildis fa faw.
The king crochit with croun, cumly and cleir,
Tuke him up by the hand,
With ane fair fembland.
Grete honour that avenand
Did to the deir.

XXIII. Than

XXIII.

Than that feymly be fight faid to the gent,
Wes vailyeand, and verteous, foroutin ony vice;
" Heir am I cumyn, at this tyme, to your prefent,
" As to the wourfchipfulleft in warld, wourthy, and wifc;
" Of al the ryngis in erd richeft of rent;
" Of pyth, and of proues, peirles of prife.
" Heir I mak you ane grant, with gudly entent,
" Ay to your prefence to perfew, with all my fervice.
" Quhare ever ye found, or fair, be firth, or be fell,
" I fal be reddy at your will,
" In alkin refonne, and fkill;
" As I am haldin thair till,
" Treuly to tell."

XXIV.

He did the conquer to knaw all the caufe quhy,
That all his hathillis in the heir hailly on hight;
How he wes wounyng of wer with WAWANE the wy;
And al the fortonne the freke befell in the fight.
The dout, and the danger, he tauld him quently.
Than faid ARTHUR him felvin, femely by fight,
" This is ane foveranefull thing, be Jhefu, think I;
" To leif in fic perell, and in fa grete plight.
" Had ony preuidice apperit, in the partyce,
" It had bene grete perell.
" Bot fen the lawté is lell,
" That thow my kyndnes wil heill,
" The mare is thi price.

XXV. " I

XXV.

" I thank the mekill, Schir Knight," said the ryal.
" It makis me blythar to be, than al thi braid landis ;
" Or all the renttis fra thyne unto *Ronfrwall,*
" Thoght I myght reif thame with right, rath to my handis."
Than said the senyeour in fyth, semely in saill,
‘ Becaufe of yone bald berne, that broght me of bandis,
‘ All that I have undir hewine I hald of you haill,
‘ In firth, foreft, and fell, quhare ever that it ftandis.
‘ Se wourfchipfull WAWANE has wonnin to your handis
‘ The fenyory in gouernyng,
‘ Cum'y conquerour, and kyng,
‘ Heir mak I you obeifing
‘ As leige lord of landis,

XXVI.

‘ And fyne fewte I you feft, without fenyeing,
‘ Sa that the caufe may be kend, and knawin throw fkill,
‘ Blithly how, and obcie to your bidding,
‘ As I am haldin to tell treuly thair till.’
Of Schir GOLOGRAS’ grant blith wes the king ;
And thoght the fordward wes fair, freyndfchip to fulfill,
Thair Schir GAWANE, the gay, throu requiring
Gart the foverane himfelf, femely on fill,
Cary to the caftel cleirly to behald,
With all the wourthy that were,
Erll, duke, and Douch fpere,
Baith banrent, and bachilere,
That blyth war and bald.

7   XXVII. Quhen

XXVII.

Quhen the femely foverane wes fet in the faill,
It wes felcouth to fe the feir fervice;
Wynis wifly in wane went full grete waill
Amang the pryncis in place, peirles to price.
It war teir for to tel treu!y in tail
To ony wy in this warld wourthy, I wife.
With revaling and revay, all the oulk hale;
Alfo rachis can ryn undir the wod rife.
On the riche river of *Rone* ryot thai maid,
And fyne, on the nynte day,
The renkis rial of array
Bownyt hame thair way
Withoutin mare baid.

XXVIII.

Quhen the ryal Roy, maift of renoune,
With al his reverend rout wes reddy to ryde;
The king, cumly with kith, wes crochit with croune,
To Schir GOLOGRAS, the gay, faid gudly that tyde;
" Heir mak I the reward, as I have refoune,
" Before their fenyeouris in fight, femely befide,
" As tuiching the temporalité in toure, and in toune,
" In firth, foreft, and fell, and woddis fo wide,
" I mak releifching of thyn allegiance.
" But dreid I fall the warand,
" Baith be fey, and be land,
" Fre, as I the firft fand,
" Withoutin diftance."

EXPLICIT.

BALADE.

BALADE,

Thingis in kynde defyris thingis lyke;
Bot difcontrair hatis ewiry thing :
Sauf onely mankinde can nevir wele lyke,
Bot gif he have a latioufe lyving.
Flefhly defyre, and gaftely nurifching,
Intill a perfone all famyn to be wrought ;
Water and fyre togeder in kyndelyng,
It may wele ryme, bot it accordis nought.

A man at one for to ferve lordis twayn,
The quhilk be baith contrair in opynion ;
To plefe thame bath, and purches no difdayn,
Talk with that ane, and with the tothir rown :
Be trew to both, without tuigh of trefon,
Tell hym of hym the thing that nevir was wrought;
To bring all this to gude conclufion,
It may wele ryme, bot it accordis nought.

To have a gall, clepit a gentill dow ;
To be my frende, and geve me falfe counfaill ;
To brek my hede, and fyne put on a how ;
To be a prefte, and formeft in bataill ;
To ly in bed, and ftrang caftell affaill ;
To be a marchand, quhare na gude may be bought ;
To have a trew wyf with a wanton taile,
It may wele ryme, byt it accordis nought.

To

To be of no conyng, and knaw the herbe ;
To carp langage that non may undirftand ;
A fule to have a veray wife proverbe ;
A fre born barne of hir that is a bonde ;
Unpoffible thingis to tak on hond ;
To big a caftell, or the ground be wrought ;
To geve a dome be law that may noght ftond ;
It may wele ryme, bot it accordis noght.

A wregh to were a nobill fcarlet goun ;
A badlyng, furryng parfillit wele with fable ;
A gude hufywyf ay rynnyng in the toun ;
A childe to thryve quhilk is unchaftiable.
To be content, and lightly changeable ;
To have in daynté thing that newir doucght ;
A Rome-rynnar without lefing or fable ;
It may wele ryme, bot it accordis noutght.

A myghty king intill a pore region ;
Ane hafty wit, and hye thingis to devife ;
Meke almoufe dede, and falfe detraction ;
Kynitghly manhede, and fchamefull couardife ;
A hevynly hell, a poynefull paradife ;
A haly doctour with a lecheroufe thought ;
To wirk on hede, fyne efter tak avife ;
It may wele ryme, bot it accordis noght.

Agilty

A gilty tong colourit with eloquence ;
A falfe entend within and diffavable ;
A blyth vifage with frendely apperence ;
A cruell hert invioufe and vengeable ;
A gentill horfe intill a nakit ftable ;
A mery fang, the hert with forow fought ;
To feme thir all, and mak thame fufficiable,
It may wele ryme, bot it accordis nought.

Frely to fpend, and full of covatife ;
To feke burgeons out of ane ald dry ftok ;
A gay temple without dyvine fervice ;
A birdles cage ; a key withoutyn lok ;
A toun fchip ay ryding in a rok ;
A myghty bifchop in a cointre of nought ;
A wantoun hird, and a wele reulit flok ;
It may wele ryme, bot it accordis nought.

    Heir endis the knightly tale of GOLAGROS and
GAWANE, in the fouth gait of Edinburgh be Walter
Chepman and Androw Millar the viii day of Aprile the
yhere of God M.ccccc and viii yheris.

BALADE I.

BALADE I*.

In all oure gardyn growis thare na floutis,
Heibe nor tre that frute hes borne this yere:
'The levys ar doun fchakyn with the fchouris;
Th fynkle fadit in oure grene herbere.
Tne birdis, that bene wount to fyngen here,
In all this May unefe has fongin thrife:
And all of dangere is oure gardenere:
And gentrife is put quite out of fervice.

Quhat that I mene be this, I dar noght fpeke,
For I na dare, my hert it is fo fare.
Na never fall I me revenge na wreke,
Bot on myfelf, allthogh I fuld forfar.
Saufand beauté I can prife na mare
Of hyr that was wont to be gudelieſt:
And futh it is and fene, in all our quhare,
No erdly thing bot for a tyme may left.

Sen in this warld thare is no fekernes,
Botand, as men all end, mon every thing is,
I tak my leve at all unftedfaftnes.

* This, and the five following ballads, are alfo printed at Edinburgh, 1508, 8vo.

BALADE II.

B A L A D E II.

Wythin a garth, under a rede rofere,
Ane ald man, and decrepit, herd I fyng;
Gay was the note, fuete was the voce, and clere,
It was grete joy to here of fic a thing.
And, to my dome, he faid in his dyting,
For to be yong I wald not for my wis,
Off all this warld to mak me lord and king.
The more of age, the nerar hevynnis blis..

Falfe is this warld, and full of variance,
Befoncht with fyn, and othir fytis mo.
Treuth is all tynt; gyle has the gouuernance;
Wrechitnes has wroht all welthis wele to wo.
Fredom is tynt, and flemyt the lordis fro;
Aud covatife is all the caufe of this.
I am content that youthede is ago.
The more of age, the nerar hevynnis bliffe.

The ftate of youth I repute for na gude,
For in that ftate fic perilis I fee;
Bot full fmal grace: the regeing of his blud
Can non gaynftand, quhill that he agit be;
Syne of the thing, that tofore joyit he,
Nothing remanys for to be callit his;
For quhy it were bot veray vanitee.
The more of age, the nerar hevynnis bliffe.

                                        Suld

Suld na man traift this wrechit warld, for quhy
Of erdly joy ay forow is the end.
The ftate of it can no man certify:
This day a king; to morn na gude to fpend.
Quhat have we here, bot grace us to defend?
The quhilk God grant us for to mend oure mys;
That to his glore he may oure faulis fend.
The more of age, the nerar hevynnis bliffe.

BALLADE III.

Devife, prowes, and eke humilitee,
That maidenis have in euerich wyfe,
Tranfmovit is in ferpentis crueltee,
Fra thay in warld be weddit wyth thir wyis.
No manis wit to wonder may fuffice
Quhare ar becumyn thir maidenis myld of mude,
Of all this wyfis that non are found gude.

O maidynhede of virtue nobileft,
Flurifching in joy, and perfyte lawlynes!
O wyfhede wariit of wyis wickiteft,
Moder of vice, and hertis hye diftreffe!
The caufe caufing of ruyne, as I geffe,
That all this warld has broght to confufion
Begonnyn was throu thy perfwafion.

Enfample is how thyne iniquitee
Ourcumyn has wyfedom, and ftrenth of hand;
Be SALOMON the firft may provit be,
Wifeft but were in warld that was lyfand,
His grete wifedome mycht not agayn thé ftand;
Thou gert hym err into his latter elde,
Declyne his God, and to the mawmentis yeld.

SAMPSON

Sampson the ſtrongeſt that ewir was borne
Off manly forſe throu the diſtroit was,
Both his eyne blyndit, and eke forlorn.
David that ſlew the gyant Golyas ;
And mony mo, the quhilk I have na ſpace
For to reheiſe, for lak of tyme and wit,
And for grete labour tharſore I mon our ſett.

Thou devillis member, thou curſit homycide,
Thou tigir tene, fulfild of birnyng fyre,
Thou ſchryne ſecrete of ſtynkand doke, and pride,
Thou cocatras, that with the ſicht of thy ire
Affrayit has full mony a gudely fyre,
That eftward in warld had newir pleſance
Grete God I pray to take on the vengeance.

In maidynhede ſen was oure firſt remede,
And fra the hevyn oure haly fader ſent
The ſecund perſone, his ſone, in a Godhede,
To tak mankynde upon the maidyn gent,
Clene of hir corſe, and clenar of entent,
That bure the barne quhilk couerit us fra care,
Scho being virgyn clenar than ſcho was are.

Grete was the luft that thou had for to fang
The frute vetit, throu thy falfe counfailing
Thou gert mankynde confent to do that wrang,
Declyne his God, and brek his hie bidding,
As haly write beris futhfaft witneffing.
Tharfor thou fro the joy of paradife,
And thyne ofspring, was banyft for thy vice.

EXPLICIT.

BALLADE IV.

B A L L A D E   IV.

Of ferlyis of this grete confufion
I wald fum clerk of conyng walde declerde;
Quhat gerris this warld be turnyt up fo doun ;
Thare is na faithfull faftnes found in erd.
Now ar.noucht thre may traiftly trow the ferde:
Welth is away, and wit is worthin wrynkis :
Now fele is forow, this is a wofull werde,
Sen want of wyfe men maks fulis to fit on binkis.

That tyme quhen [rang] the lovit king SATURNUS,
For gudely governance this warld was goldin cald ;
For untreuth we wate noucht quhare to it turnis.
The tyme that OCTOVIAN the monarch could hald,-
Our all was pes, wele fet as hertis wald ;
Than regnyt reule, and refon held his rynks.
Now lakkis prudence; nobilitee is thralde,
Sen want of wyfe men makis fulis to fitt on bynkis.

ARESTOTILL for his moralitee,
AUSTYN, or AMBROSE for dyvine fcripture ;
Quha can _placebo_, and noucht half _dirigs_,
That praftik for to pike, and pill, the pure ;
He fall cum in, and thay ftand at the dure.
For warldly wynfik walkis, quhen wyfar wynkis :
Wit takis na worfchip, fic is the aventure,
Sen want of wyfe men makis fulis to fitt on binkis.

K 3   Now,

Now, but defenſe, rycht lyis all deſolate,
Rycht na reſon, under na rufe has reſt.
Youth is but raddour, and age is obſtynate,
Mycht but mercy, the pore ar all oppreſt.
Lerit folk ſuld tech the peple of the beſt,
Thouch lare be lytill, fer leſſe in tham ſinkis.
It may noucht be this warld ay thus ſuld leſt,
That want of wyſe men makis fulis ſitt on binkis.

For now is exilde all ald noble corage,
Lautee, lufe, and liberalitee.
Now is ſtabilitee fundyn in na ſtage,
Nor digeſt counſele wyth ſad maturitee.
Peas is away ail in perplexitee ;
Prudence, and policy, are banyſt our al brinkis.
This warld is ver ſa may it callit be,
That want of wife men makis fulis ſitt on bynkis.

Quhare is the balance of juſt and equitee ?
Nothir meryt is preiſit, na punyſt is treſpas.
All ledis lyvis lawles at libertee,
Nouch reulit be reſon, mare than ox, or aſſe.
Gude faith is flemyt, worthin fraillar than glas ;
Trew lufe is lorn, and lautee haldis no lynkis ;
Sic gouuernance I call noucht a faſſe,
Sen want of wife men makis fulis ſitt on binkis.

O Lord

O Lord of Lordis! God and Governour!
Makar, and movar, bath of mare and leſſe!
Quais power wiſedome and honoure
Is infynite, ſal be, and ewirwas wes,
As in the principall mencion of the meſſe,
All thir ſayd thingis reform, as thou beſt thinkis,
Quhilk ar degradit for pure pitee redreſſe,
Sen want of wiſe men makis fulis fit on biukis.

BALLADE V.

B A L L A D E V.

The ballade of ane right noble, victorius, and myghty lord, BARNARD STEWART, Lord of AUBIGNY, Erle of BEAUMONT, ROGER, and BONAFFRE, Confalour and Chamberlane ordinare to the maift hee, maift excellent, and maift cryftyn prince, LOYS King of France, Knight of his Ordoure, Capitane of the kepyng of his Body, Conqueror of Naplis, and um- quhile Conftable General of the fame; Compilit be Maiftir WILLYAM DUMBAR, at the faid lordis cumyng to Edinburghe in Scotland, fend in ane ryght excellent embaffat fra the faid maift Cryftin King to our maift fouerane lord, and victorious prince, James the Ferde, Kyng of Scottis. [1503.]

Renownit, ryall, right reverend, and ferene,
Loid hie tryumphing in wirfchip and valoure,
Fro kyngis downe moft criftin knight, and kene,
Moft wyfe, moft valyand, mofte laureat hie wictoure.
Onto the fterris upheyt is thyne honour!
In Scotland welcum be thyne excellence
To King, Queyne, lord, clerk, knight, and fervatour,
Withe glorie and honour, lawde and reverence.

Welcum in ftour moft ftrong, incomparable knight,
The fame of armys, and floure of vaffalage.
Welcum in were moft worthi, wyfe and wight;
Welcum the foune of Mars of moft curage.

Welcum

Welcum mofte lufti branche of our linnage,
In every realme oure fcheild, and our defence;
Welcum our tendir blude of hie parage,
With glorie and honour, lawde and reverence.

Welcum in were the fecund JULIUS,
The prince of knightheyd, and flour of chevalry,
Welcum moft valyeant and victorius,
Welcum invincible victour, mofte wourthy.
Welcum our Scottis chiftane moft dughti,
Wyth fowne of clarioun, organe, fong, and fence.
To the atonis, lord, welcum all we cry,
With glorie and honour, lawde and reverence.

Welcum our indeficient adjutorie,
That ever our naceoun helpit in thare neyd,
That never faw Scot yit indigent nor fory,
Bot thou did hym fuport with thi gud deid.
Welcum therfor abufe all levand leyd,
Withe us to live, and to maik recidence,
Quhilk never fall fwnye for thi faik to bleid,
To quham be honour, lawde and reverence.

Is none of Scotland borne fathfull and kynde,
Bot he of naturall inclinacioune
Dois favour thé withe all his hert and mynde,
Withe fervent, tendir, trew, intencioun;

And

And wald of inwart hie effeftioun,
But dreyd of danger, de in thi defence,
Or dethe, or fchame, war done to thi perfoun,
To quhame be honour, lawde and reverence.

Welcum thow knight mofte fortunable in feild,
Welcum in armis moft aunterus and able,
Wndir the fown, that beris helme or fcheild;
Welcum thow campioun, in fight wnourcumable.
Welcum moft dughti, digne and honorable,
And moift of lawde, and hie magnificence;
Nixt wndir Kingis to ftand incomparable,
To quham be honour, lawde and reverence.

Throw Scotland, Ingland, France, and Lumbardy,
Fleys on weyng thi fame, aud thi renoune,
And our all cuntreis wndirnethe the fky,
And our all ftrandis fro the fterris doune.
In every province, land, and regioun,
Proclamit is thi name of excellence;
In every ceté, village, and in toune,
Withe gloire and honour, lawde and reverence.

O feyrfe ACHILL in furius hie curage!
O ftrong invincible HECTOR undir fcheild!
O vailyeant ARTHUR in knyghtli vaffalage!
AGAMEMNON in governance of feild!

Bold

Bold Hynniball in batall to do beild!
Julius in jupert, in wifdom and expence!
Maft fortunable chiftane bothe in yhouth and eild!
To the be honour, lawde and reverence.

At parlament thou fuld be hye renownit,
That did fo mony victoryfe opteyn.
Thi criftall helme withe lawry fuld be crownyt,
And in thi hand a branche of olyve greyn.
The fueird of conquis and of knyghteid keyn
Be borne fuld highe before thé in prefence,
To reprefent fic man as thou has beyn,
With glorie and honour, lawde and reverence.

Hie furius Mars, the god armipotent,
Rong in the hevin at thyne nativité;
Saturnus doune withe fyry eyn did blent,
Throw bludy vifar, men manafing to gar dé.
On thé frefche Wenus keift hir amouroufe e;
On thé Marcurius furtheyet his eloquence;
Fortuna Major did turn hir face on thé,
With glorie and honour, lawde and reverence.

Prynce of fredom, and flour of gentilnes,
Sweyrd of knightheid, and chaife of chevalry,
This tyme I lefe, for grete prolixitnes,
To tell quhat feildis thow wan in Pikkardy,

In

In France, in Bertan, in Naplis, and Lumbardy ;
As I think eftir, withe all my diligence,
Or thow departe at lenthe for to difcry,
With glorie and honour, lawd and reverence.

B in thi name betaknis batalrus ;
A able in feild ; R right renoune moft hie ;
N nobilnes ; and A for aunterus ;
R ryall blude ; for dughtenes is D ;
W valyeantnes ; S for ftrenewite ;
Quhoife knyghtli name, fo fchynyng in clemence,
For wourthines in gold fuld writtin be,
With glorie and honour, lawde and reverence.

*   *   *   *   *
*   *   *   *   *
*   *   *   *   *

Several Pages are here wanting.

BALLADE VI.

BALLADE VI.

My gudame wes a gay wif, bot fcho wes ryght gend;
Scho dvelt furth fer into [Fyfe*] apon *Falkland fellis*;
Thai callit [her] kynd KITTOK, quhafa hir weill kend;
Scho wes like a caldrone cruke, cler under kellys.
Thai threpit that fcho eit of thrift; and maid a gude end.
Eftir hir dede fcho dredit nought in hevin for to duell:
And fa to hevin the hieway dreidles fcho wend,
Yit fcho wandit, and yeid by to ane elriche well.
Scho met thar, as I wene,
Ane afk rydand on a fnaill,
And cryit, "Ourtane fallow haill!"
And raid ane inche behind the taill,
Till it wes neir evin.

Sa fcho had hap to be horfit to hir herbry,
Att ane ailhous neir, it nyghttit thaim thare.
Scho deit of thrift in this warld that gert hir be fo dry,
Scho neuer eit bot drank our mefure and mair.
Scho flepit quhill the morne at none, and rais airly,
And to the yeƈtis of hevin faft can the wif fair,
And by Sanƈt Petir, in at the yet fcho ftall prevely.
God lukit and faw hir lattin in, and lewch his hert fair.
And thar, yeris fevin,
Scho lewit a gud lif;
And wes our ladyis hen-wif;
And held Sanƈt Peter at ftrif,
Ay quhill fcho wes in hevin.

* In the original *France*; a typographical error.

Sche

Sche lukit out on a day, and thogt ryght lang,
To fe the ailhous befide, intill ane evill hour;
And out of hevin the hie gait cought the wif gaing,
For to get hir ane frefche drink, the aill of hevin wes four.
Scho come agane to hevinis yer, quhen the bell rang,
Saint Petir hat hir with a club, quhill a grete clour
Rais in hir heid, becaus the wif yeid wrang.
Than to the ailhous agane fcho ran, the pycharis to pour;
And for to brew, and baik.
Frendis, I pray yow hertfally,
Gif ye be thrifty, or dry,
Drink with my guddame, as ye ga by,
Anys for my faik.

APPENDIX;

CONTAINING

THREE PIECES

BEFORE UNPUBLISHED.

THE

H O U L A T,

OR

THE DANGER OF PRIDE.

A FABLE.

IN THREE PARTS.

――――――

PART I.

―――

ARGUMENT.

THE Poet walks by a river, in May, *Stanza* i.—Plea-
fures of the place, ii, .iii.—A houlat, or owl, appears
in a holly, looking at her image in the water, iv.—
Complaint of the owl, v.—He refolves to appeal to
the Pope againft Nature, vi.—The owl requefts the
peacock, the Pope of birds, to be made fair, vii, viii.
ix.—A council of birds fummoned, x—xix.—They
argue upon the cafe, and, as it is temporal, fubmit it
to the Emperor, xx—xxiii.—The eagle, or Emperor,
goes to the council, and his attendants, xxiv.

THE

H O U L A T E.

MAID BE HOLLAND.

———————

I.

IN the middis of Maii, at morne, as I went,
Throw mirth markit on mold, till a grene meid,
The blemis blyweft of blee fro the fone blent,
· That all brychnit about the bordouris on breid.
With alkin herbis off air that war in erd lent
The feildis flowryfchit, and fretfull of fairheid.
So foft was the feafons our fourane doun fent,
Throw the greabill gift off his godheid,
That all was amiable ower the air and the erd.
Thus throw the clifts fo clere
Above, but fallow or fere,
I waikit till a riweir
That ryallye rered.

II. This

II.

This riche rywer down ran, but refting or rove,
Throw a foreft on fauld, that ferlye was fair.
All the brayis of that buyrne buir brenchis above;
And birdis blyitheft of ble on bloffomes bair.
The land lony was, and lie, with lyking and love.
And for to lende by that läk thocht me levare,
Becaufs that thir hertis in herdis coud hove;
Pranfaod and pridyeand, be pair and be pare.
Thus fat I in folace, fekrelye and fuire,
Content of the fare firth,
Mekle mare of the mirth;
Als was blyith of the birth,
That the ground buire.

III.

The birth that the ground bure was brondyn in bredis,
With gerfs gay as the gold, and granis of grace,
Mendis and medicine for all menis (neidis *;)
Heip till hert, and till hurt, helefull it was.
Under the circle folar thir fanourous fedis
Were nurift be dame Nature, that nobill maiftres.
Bot all thair namys to nyum as now it nocht nedis;
It wer prolixit and lang, and lenthing of fpace.
And I haif mekle matter in metir to glofs,
Of ane uthir fentence;
And waik is my eloquence.
Thairfoir in haift will I hence
To the purpofe.

* leydis, *MS. margin.*

IV.

Of that purpois in that place, be pryme of the day,
I hard a peteous appeill, with a pure mane,
Sowlpit in forrow, that fadly could fay,
" Woes me wreche in this warld wilfum of wane!"
With mair murnyng, in mynd than I mene may;
Rowpit rewchfully roulk in a rud rane,
Off that ferly on fold I fell in affray.
Nyrar that noyris in neft I nycht in ane,
I faw a HOULAT in haift, under ane holyng,
Lukand the lak throw,
And faw hir awin fhadow,
At the quhilk he culd grow,
And maid a gowling.

V.

He gret gryflie grym, and gaif a grit youle,
Hedand and hydand with churlich chere.
" Quhy is my fate," quoth the fyle, " faffeint fo foule?
" My forme, and my fetherin, unfrelie but feir;
" My neb is nytherit as a nob. I am but ane oule.
" Againis natur in the nycht I waik into weir.
" I dar do nocht in the day bot droup as a doule;
" Nocht for fhame of my fhaip in pert till appeir.
" Thus all the foulis, for my filth, hes me at feid;
" That be I fene in thair ficht
" To luke out on day lycht,
" Sum will me dolefully dycht,
" Sum dring me to my deid.

L 3   VI. " Sum

VI.

" Sum bird will bay at my beke, and fum will me byte;
" Sum fkirp me with fcorne, fum fkyrine at myn e.
" I fee be my fhaddow my fhap hes the wyte.
" Quhame fall I bleme in this breth, a befum that I be ?
" Is none bot dame Natur I bid not to wyte
" To accufs, in this caufs, in cais that I de.
" Bot quha fall make me amendis of hir worth a myte,
" That this hes maid on the mold a monfter of me ?
" I will appeill to the Paip, and pafs to him plane ;
" For happin that his halynace,
" Throw prayer, may purchace
" To reforme my foule face ;
" And than wer I fane.

VII.

" Fane wald [I ken], quoth the fyle, or I furth fure,
" Quha is fader of all foule, paftour and Paip ?
" That is the plefand *Pacok*, pretious and pure,
" Conftant and kirklyk, under his cleir kaip;
" Myterit, as the maner is, manfuiet and demure;
" Schrowd in his fcheneweid, and fchane in his fchaip;
" Sad in his fanctitude, fickerly and fure.
" I will go to that guid, his grace for to graip."
Off that boure I was blyeth ; and baid to behald.
The *Howlate*, violent of vyce,
Raikit under the ryce,
To the *Pacok* of pryce,
That was Pape cald.

VIII. Beffoir

VIII.

Beffoir the Paip quhen that puir prefent him had,
With fit courtaffye, as he coud, on knees he fell.
Said, "*Ave* Rabye ! Be the rude I am rych rade,
" To behald your Hellynes, or my taill tell.
" I may nocht fuffife to fe your Sanctitude fad."
The Paip wyiflie, I wis, of wirfchip the well,
Gawe him his braid bennefoun } and balelie him bade,
That he fuld fpeanlie fpeik, and fpair nocht to fpell.
" I com to fpeir," quoth the fpreit, " into fpeciall,
" Quhy I am formit fa foull ;
" Ay to yout and to youll,
" As ane horuble oull,
" Ougfum owir all ?

IX.

" I am nycherit ane oule thus be Nature,
" Lykar a fulle, than a foul!, in figure and face.
" Byffym of all birdis, that evir bodye bure,
" Without caws or cryme kend in this cace.
" I have appeillit to your prefence, pretious and puir,
" To afk help into haift at your Holynace,
" That ye wald crye upoun Chrift, that all hes in cuir,
" To fchaƿe me ane fchand bird in a fchort fpace.
" And to accufe Nature this is no uay.
" Thus throw your Halynes may ye
" Make a fair foull ot me ;
" Or ellis dreidles I dee,
" Or my end day."

X.

'Off thy deid,' quoth the Paip, ' pitie I hawe ;
' Bot of Nature to pleyne it is pariell.
' I can nocht fay fuddanlie, fo me Chrift fawe,
' Bot I fall call my cardinallis, and my counfell.
' Patriarkis and prophetis, oure lerit all the lawe,
' Thai fal be femblit full fone, that thow fe fall.'
He callit on his Cubiculare within his conclawe
That was the proper *Pape*, proud in his apparrell :
Bad fend for his fecretare, and his fele fone,
That was the *Turture* treweft
Ferme, faithfull, and feft,
That bure that office honeft ;
And enterit but hone.

XI.

The Paip commandit, but hone, to wryt in all landis,
Be the faid fecretare, that the fele yemyt,
For all ftaitis of kirk, that under Chrift ftandis,
To femble till his fummondis, as it weill femyt.
The trew *Turture* has tane with the titgandis,
Done dewly his dett as the dere demyt :
Syne belyve fend the lettres into fere landis,
With the *Swallow* fo fwift in fpeanle expremit,
The Papis herald at poynt into prefent ;
For he is furthward to flee,
And ay will haif enteree
In hous, and in hall hee,
To tell his entent.

XII. Quhat

XII.

Quhat fall I tell ony mair of thir materis?
· Bot thir lordis belyve thir lettres hes tane,
Reffavit thame with reverence, to reid as efferis;
And richelye the heraldis rewardit ilk ane.
Than bufk thai but blin; monye bewfckeris
Graithis thame, but growching, that gait for to gane.
All the ftaitis of kirk out of fteid fteris:
And I fall note you richt now thair namis in ane.
How thai apperit to the Paip, and prefent thame ay;
Fair farrand, and free,
In ane guidlye degree,
And manlyke; as thocht me
In middis of May.

XIII.

All thus in May, as I went in a morning,
Come foure *Phefandis* full fair, in the firft front;
Prefentit thame as Patriarkis in thair appering,
Benygne of obedience, and blyith in the bront.
A college of Cardinallis come fyne in a ling,
That war *Crannis* of kynd gif I rycht compt; ·
With ride hattis on heid in hale carkining
Off that deir dignitie, with wirfchip ay wont.
Thir ar foulis of effect, but felonye or feid,
Spiritual in all thing
Leill in thair leving;
Thairfore in dignitie ding
Thai ding to thair deid.

XIV. Yit

XIV.

Yit induring the day to that dere drew
Swannis fwonchand full fwyith, fweiteft of fware;
In quhite rokattis,arrayit, as I rycht knew,
That thai wer Byfhopp:s blift I was the blyvare.
S able, and fteidfaft, tender and trew;
Off few wordis, full wyifs and worthye, thai ware.
Thair was *Pyattis*, and *Pertrekis*, and *Plevaris* anew,
As abbatis of all ordouris that honorable ar.
The *See mawis* war monkis, the blak and the qubyte.
The *Goull* was a garnitar,
The *Swerthbak* a fcellerar,
The *Scarth* a fyfh-fangar,
And that a perfyte.

XV.

Perfytelie thir *Pik mawis* as for priouris,
With thair partie habitis, prefent thame thair.
Herronis contemplative clein chentouris
With toppit hudes on heid, and cleir of hair.
A7 forrowfull and faid at all houris;
Was never leid faw thame lauch; bot drow pane and dare.
All kin chennonis eik of uthir ordouris;
All manor of religioun, the lefs and the mair.
Cryand *Crawis*, and *Kais*, and that crewis the corne,
War puir frewp forward
That with the leve of the lard,
Will into the corne yard
At evin and at morne.

XVL Yet

XVI.

Yet or evin enterit that bure offyce,
Obeyand thir Bifchoppis, and bydand thame by,
Grit *Ganaris* on ground, in gudlie awyce,
That war demit but dout Denys duchty.
Thai mak reference rith, and airlie will ryifs
To keip the college clein, and the clargye.
The *Roke* in his cleir caip, that crawis and cryis,
Was chofen Chantor full cheif in the chenonrye.
Thair cum the *Curllew* a Clark, and that a cunand,
Chargit as chancellare,
For he could wryte wonder fare,
With his neb for myftar
Upoun the fee fand.

XVII.

Upoun the fand that I faw, as the fanrare tane,
With grene awmons on hede, Sir Gawane the *Drake*;
The *Arfeene* that our man ay prichand in plane,
Correétor of Kirkine was clepit the *Clake.*
The *Morton*, the *Murecok*, the *Myrfnyp* in ane,
Lychtir, as lerit men of law, by that lake.
The *Ravin*, rowpand rudely in a roch rane,
Was Dene rurall to rede rank as a rake ;
Quhill the lardun was laid, held he na houfs ;
Bot in uplandis townis
At Vicaris and Perfonis,
For the procurationis
Cryand full croufs.

XVIII. The

XVIII.

The croufs *Capon*, a Clerk under cleir wedis,
Full of cherité, chafte and unchangeable,
Was Officiale but les that the law ledis
In caufis confiftorial, that ar courfable.
The *Sparrow* veug he vefyit for his vile dedis,
Lyand in lechorye, lafch, unlouable.
The *Feldefar*, in the forreft that febily him fedis,
Be ordour ane hofpitular was ordanit full hable.
The *Kowfchots* war Perfonis in thair apparrele.
The *Dow* NOYES meffingere,
Rownand ay with his fere
Was a Curate, to here
Confeffionis hale.

XIX.

Cenfefs cleir can I nocht, nor kyth all the cas,
The kynd of thair cunnyng, thir compargés eke;
The manere, nor the multitude fomonyt than was.
All fe foull, and fede foull, was nocht for to feke.
Thir ar no foulis of ref, nor of rethnas,
Bot manfuete, but malice, mandrit and meke,
And all apperit to the Paip, in that ilk place,
Saluft his fanctitude with fpirituall fpeke.
The Pape gaif his benefon, and bliffit thame all.
Quhen thai war rankit on rawis
Off thair wing, the haill cawis
Was faid into fchort fawis,
As ye here fail.

XX. The

XX.

The Pape faid to the *Oule*, "Propone thine appele,
"Thy lamentabill langage, as lyke the beft."
' I am defcernint of the foul, with faltis full fele,
' Be nature nycherit ane oule noy quhar in neft,
' Wrech of all wrechis, fra wirfchip and wele ;
(All this tretye hes he tald be times inteft.)
' It nedis nocht to renew all my unhele,
' Sen it was menit to your mynd, and maid manifeft.',
Bot to the poynt pietous he prait the Pape
To call the clergye with cure
And fe gif that Nature
Mycht reforme his figure
In a fair fchaip.

XXI.

Than fairly the Fader thir foulis he frainyt
Off thair cunfele in this cais, fen that the rycht knew ;
Gyff thai the *Houlat* mycht help, that was fo hard panyt.
And thai verelye avifit, full of vertewe,
The mater, the manner, aud how it remanyt ;
The circumftance, and the ftait, all coude thai argewe.
Monye alleageance lele, in lede nocht to laneit,
Off ARISTOTLE, aud all men, fchairplye thai fchewe.
The prelatis thair apperance proponit generall.
Sum faid to, fum fra ;
Sum nay, and fum ya.
Baith *pro* and *contra*
Thus argewe thai all.

XXII. Thus

XXII.

Thus argewe thai erniftlye wone offis ;
And fyn to the famyn forfuth thai affent hale ;
That fen it nychlit Nature, thair alleris maiftris,
Thai coud nocht trete but entent of the temperale.
Thairfore thai counfele the Pape to wryte on this wys,
To the achil Emprour, fouerane in fale,
Till addrefs to that diete, to deme his avis,
With Dukis, and with digne Lordis, derreft in dale,
Eriis of anceftry, and uthir ynewe.
So that Spirituale State
And the feculare confate,
Mycht all gang in a gate
Tendir and trewe.

XXIII.

The trew *Turture*, and traift, as I heire tald,
Wrate thir lettres at lenth, leleft in lede ;
Syne throw the Papis pretext planelye thame yald
To the *Swallow* fo fwift, harrald in hede,
To ettill to the Emproure, of anceftry ald.
He wald nocht fpare for to fpring on a hind fpede :
Fand him in *Babilonis tour*, with bernis fa bald,
Cruell kingis with crouns, and ducks but drede.
He gave thir lordis belyve the lettres to luke ;
Quhilk the riche Emproure,
And all other in the houre
Reffavit with honour,
Bayth Princis, and Duke.

XXIV. Quhen

XXIV.

Quhen thai confavit had the cas, and the credence,
Be the herald in hall hufe thai nocht ellis,
Bot bownis out of *Babilon* with all obedience,
Sekis our the falt fee, fro the fouth fellis,
Enteris in *Europ*, free but offence,
Waillis wylie the wayis, be woddis and wellis,
Till thai approch to the Pape in his prefence,
At the foirfaid trifte quhar the treté tellis.
Thai fand him in a forreft, frelye and fare.
Thay halfit his Halynes.
And ye fall here, in fchort fpace,
Quhat worthy Lordis thair was,
Giff your willis ware.

PART II.

PART II.

ARGUMENT.

The birds of prey, &c. who attend the emperor, I, II.—
The poet goes into a ſtrange digreſſion, for the remainder
of this Part, and deſcribes the arms of the Pope, the
Emperor, and France, III, IV.—Thoſe of Scotland,
and of Douglas, V, VI.—The green tree of Douglas,
its four branches, and arms of each, VII, VIII.—The
cauſes and origin of the arms of Douglas, IX, X,
XI.—The expedition of Douglas to the Holy Land
with the heart of Robert I. XII—XVIII.—The ſtars
and other arms of Douglas, XIX—XXV.

I.

Thair was the *Egill* ſo grym, gretteſt on ground is,
Achill Emproure our all, moſt awfull in erd.
Ernis ancient of air Kingis that crounid is,
Next his Celſitude forſuth fecound apperd:
Quhilk in the firmament throw fors of thair flycht found is,
Percying the forme, withyn fycht felcouth to herde.
Eyre Falcons, that gentillie in bewtye abondis,
War dere Duckis, and digne, to deme as efferd.
The *Falcon,* faireſt of flycht formyt on fold,
Was ane Erle of honour,
Marſchall to the Emprour,
Both in hall, and in bour,
Hende to behold.

II. G-

II.

Goſhalkis wer governors of thair grit oſt,
Choſin chiftanis, chevelrufs in chairges of weiris,
Marchrous in the map-mond, and of mycht moſt,
Nixt Dukis in dignité, quhome no dreid deiris.
Sperk Halkis, that ſpedely will compas the coſt,
Wer kene Knychtis of kynd, clene of maneiris,
Blyth bodeit, and beild, but barrat or boſt,
With ene celeſtiall to ſe, circulit with ſapheiris.
The *Specht* wes a Purſovand, proud to appeir,
That raid befoir the Emperour,
In a cote of armour
Of all kynd of culloar,
Cumly and cleir.

III.

He bure cumly to knaw be confcience their *
Thre cronis, and a crucifix, all of clene gold ;
The burd with orient perle plant till appeir,
Dicht as a dyademe digne, deir to behold,
Archt on ilka ſyd with a ſapheir,
The jaſpirs jonit the jem, and rubeyis inrold.
Syne twa keys our corfs, of ſilver ſo cleir †,
In a field of aſur flamit on fold ;
The Paipis armis at poynt to blaſone and beir,
As feiris for a Purſovant,
That will viage avant ;
Active, and avenant,
Armes to weir.

* The armes. *MS. margin.*   † Paipis armes. *ib.*

IV.

Syne in a field of filuer, fecound he beiris *,
Ane Egill ardent of air, that ettiles fo he;
The memburs of the famyn foule difplayit as affeiris,
Ferme formit on fold, ay fet for to fle;
All of fable the felf, quha the futh leiris,
The beke bypticit bryme of that ilk ble.
The Emprior of *Almane* tha armes he weiris,
As fignifer foverane. And fyne culd I fe †
The flour delycis of *France*, all of fyne gold,
In a field of afure,
The third armes in honour,
The faid purfevand bure
Thate blenkit fo bold.

V.

Thairwith linkit in a lyng, be leirit men approvit ‡,
He bure a lyoin as lord, of gowlis full gay,
Maid maikles of mycht, on mold quhare he movit,
Rycht rampand as Roy ryell of array.
Of pure gold wes the grund, quhair the grym hovit;
With dowble treffour about, flowrit in fay;
And flourdelycis on loft, that mony leid lovit;
Off gold figuet, and fet, to fchaw in affay.

* Emp'rs armes. *MS. margin.*
† France armes. *ib.*
‡ Scotlandis armes. *ib.*

Our fouerane in *Scotlandis* armes to knaw,
Quhilk fal be Lord and Ledar
Of bred *Britane* all quhair,
As Sanct Margaretis air,
And the fryme fhaw. .

VI.

Next the Souerane figue wes fickerly fene *,
That fermit his ferenitie ever formable,
The armes of the DowGLAS's duchty bedene,
Knawin throw all Chriftendome be cognofcence hable.
Off Scotland the weir-wall, wit ye but wene,
Our f is forfes to defend, and unfelyeable;
Baith barnekin and bar to *Scottis* blud bene,
Our lofes, and our liking, that lyne honorable.
That word is fo wondir warme, and evir yit was,
It fynkis fome in all pairt
Off a trew *Scottis* hairt,
Rewfcand us in vairt
To heir of DowGLAS.

VII.

Off the duchtie DowGLAS to dyte I me drefs;
Thair aimes of anceftre honorable ay,
Quhilk oft blithit the BRUCE in diftrefs,
Thairfoir he bliffit that blud bald in affay.

---

* The defcription of the Douglas' armes. *MS. margin.*

Reid the writ of thare werk to your witnefs,
Sin on my mater to mufe. I move as I may.
The fone Purfevand gyd wes grathit I ges,
Brufit with a greine tre, gudly and gay *;
That bure branchis on bred blytheft of hew;
Quhilk bewch to imbras
Writtin in a bill was,
O DOWGLAS, DOWGLAS,
TENDIR AND TREW !

VIII.

Syne fchyre fchapin to fchaw, mony fchene fcheild †
With tufheis of tueft filk ticht to the tre;
Ilk brenche had the berle, birth burly and beild,
Sone flureft on riall gritteft of gre.
And in the crop heich, as cheif I beheld,
Quhilk bur into afure, blytheft of ble,
Silver fternis fd fair ; and parte of the feild
Was filver fett with a hairt, heirly and he,
Of gowlis full gratnis, that glemit full gay.
Syne in afure the mold
A lyoun, cronit with gold,
Of filver ye fe fchold
To ramp in array.

* The grene tre. *MS. margin.*
† Four branches of the tre. *ib.*

IX. Quhilk

IX.

Quhilk cuffin be conyfance quartrly was,
With barris of beft gold it brint as the fyre;
And uthir fingis, forfuth furdre I gefs,
Of metteles and cullours in lentfull attyre.
It wer lere for to tell, dyte, or addrefs,
All thair deir armes in dolic defyre.
But parte of the principale neverthelefs
I fall haiftine to chew hairtly but hyre.
Thair loff and thair lordfchip of fo lang date,
That bene cot armor of eld,
Thair into herald I held ;
But fen thai the Bruce beld,
I wret as I wate.

X.

In the takin of trewth, and conftance kend,
The cullour of afure, hevinly hew,
Forthy to the Dowglas that fenye wes fend,
As leleft, all *Scotland* fra fkath to refkew.
The filver in the famyn half, trewly to tend,
Is cleir curage in armes, quha the richt knew.
The bludy hairt that he beirs the Bruce of his end,
With his eftaites in the fteid, and Nobilles enew,
Addit in the armes, for honorable caufs,
As his tendereft and deir,
In his maift mifteir ;
As fal be faid to you heir
Into fchort fawis.

XL The

XI.

The Roy ROBERT the BRUCE to raik he avowit,
· With all the hairt that he had, to the haly grave;
Syne quhen the date of his deid derfly him dowit,
With lords of *Scotland*, lerit, and the lave,
As worthy, wifeft to waile, in wirfchip allowit,
To JAME· Lord of DOWGLAS thay the gre gave,
To go with the Kingis hairt. Thairwith he nocht growit;
Bot faid to his Souerane, "So me God fave!
" Your grete giftis, and grant ay gratnis I fand;
" Bot now it moves all thir maift,
" That your hairt nobilleit
" To me is clofit and keft
" Throw your command.

XII.

" I love yow mair for that lofe ye lippen me till,
" Than ony lordfchip or land, fo me our Lorde leid!
" I fall waynd for no way to wirk as ye will,
" At wifs, gife my werd wald, with yow to the deid."
Thairwith he lowttit full law. Thame lykit full ill,
Fayth Lordis and Ladeis, that ftud in the fteid.
Off comoun natur the courfs be kynd to fulfill,
The gud King gaif the geft to God for to rede;
In *Cardrofs* that Crownit clofit his end.
Now God, for his grit grace,
Set his faule in folace!
And we will fpeik of DOWGLACE,
Quhat wey he coud weïd.

XIII. The

XIII.

The hairt coiftly he could clofs in a cleir cace,
And held alhaill the beheft he hecht to the King :
Come to the haly grave, throw Godis grit grace,
With offerandis, and orifonis, and all uthir thing ;
Our falvators fepulcour, and the famyn place,
Quhare he raifs, as we reid, richtous to ring ;
With all the relikis rath, that in that rowm wace,
He gart hallow the hairt, and fyne cud hit hing,
About his hals full hend, and on his awin hart.
Of. wald he kifs it, and cry
" O flour of chevelry !
" Quhy leif I, allace ! quhy ?
" And thow deid art !

XIV.

" My deir," quoth the DowGLAS, "art thow to deid dicht ?
" My fingular Soverane, of *Saxonis* the wand !
" Now bot I femble for thy fawlis with *Sarazenis* mycht,
" Sall I nevir fene be into *Scotland*."
Than in defens of the faith he fure to the ficht,
With knychtis of Chriftindome to keip his command.
And quhen the battellis fo bryn, brathly and blicht, ;
Were jonit thraly in thrang, mony thowfand ;
Amang the hethin men the hairt hardely he flang,
Sayd, " WEND ON, AS THOU WONT,
" THROW THE BATTEL IN BRONT ;
" AY FORMEST IN THE FRONT
" THY FATIS AMANG.

M 4   XV. " And

XV.

" And I fall fallow thé in faith, or with fayis be fellit;
" As thy lege man lele, my lyking thow art."
Thairwith on *Mahonis* men manly he mellit,
Braid throw the battelis in bront, and bur thame bakwart.
The wayis quhair the wicht went wer in wa wellit;
Wes nane fa fture in the fteid mycht ftand him aftart.
Thus frayis he the fals folk, trewly to tell it,
Ay quhill he coverit and come to the Kingis hart.
Thus fell feildis he wan ay wirchipand it.
Throwout Criftindome kid
Wer the deidis he did:
Till on a tyme it betyd,
As tellis the writ.

XVI.

He bownit to a battel, and the beld wan,
Ourfett on the Sathanas fide *Sarazenis* micht:
Syne followit faft on the chace, quhen thay fle can,
Full ferly fele hes he fellit, and flane in ficht.
As he relevit was, fo wes he ever than,
Off a wycht him allane, wirthy and wicht,
Circlit with *Sarazenis* mony a fad man,
That trawyntit with a trane upoun that trew Knycht.
" Thow fall nocht de the allane," quoth the Douglace.
" Sen I fe the ourfett,
" To fecht for the faith fett
" I fall dewoyd the of dett,
" Or de in this place." *k*

XVII. He

XVII.

He ruſchit in the grit rowt, the Knycht to reſkew,
Fell of the falſs folk, that fled of befoir,
Relevit in on thir twa, for to tell trew,
That thai war baith fainy ourſett; thairfoir I murne ſoir.
Thus in defence of the faith, as fermes anew,
And pite of the pretius Knycht that wes in yane thore,
The duchty Dowglas is deid doun adew,
With lof and with liking, that leſlis evir more.
His hardy men tuk the hairt ſyne upoun hand.
Quhen thay had bureit thair Lord,
With mekle mane to remord,
Thay maid it hame be reſtord
Into *Scotland.*

XVIII.

Be this reſone we reid, as our Roy lenit,
The Dowglas in armes the bludy hairt beiris.
For it bled he his blud, as the bill brenit:
And in batellis full bred, under baneris,
Throw full chevelrous chance he this hart chenit,
Fra walit wayis, and wicht wirthy in weiris.
Mony galyard grome wes on the grund lenit,
Quhen he it flang in the field fellon of feiris,
Syne reſkowand agane the hethin menis harmys.
This hart, red to behald,
Throw thir reſſonis ald,
The bludy harte it is cald
In Dowglas's armes.

XIX. The

XIX.

The fternis of ane uther firynd fteris fo fair *,
And callit MURRAY the riche, lord of renownis,
Deit, and a dochier had to his deir air,
Off all his trefor untald, touris and tounis.
The DowGLAS in thay dayis, duchtye Dguhare,
ARCHIBALD the honorable in habitationis,
Weddit that wlowk wicht, worthye of ware,
With rent and with riches. And be thai reffonis
He bure the fternis of eftate in his fiele wedis;
Blithe, blomand, and brycht
Throw the MURRAYIS mycht.
And fo throw Goddis foirfycht,
The DowGLAS fuccedis.

XX.

The lyoun laufand on loft, lord in effere †,
For guid caufs, as I ges, is of *Galway*.
Quhen thai rebellit the croun; and caus the King dere,
He gave it to the DowGLAS, heretabill ay:
On this wifs gif he coud win it of were;
Quhilk for his fouranis faik he fet to affay;
Kellit doun his capitanis, and could it aquere;
Maid it ferme, as we find, to our *Scottis* fay.
Thairfoir the lyoun he bure, with loving and lofs,
Of filver, femely and fur,
In a fcild of afur,
Crownit with gold pur
To the purpofs.

* The fternis. *MS. margin.*   † Lyoun. *ib.*

XXI. The

XXI.

The forreſt of *Etrik*, and uthir ynew
The landis of *Lauder*, and lordſchipis feir,
With dynt of his derf fourd the DOWGLAS ſo dew
Wan wichtly of weir, wit ye but weir,
Fro ſonis of *Saxonis*. Now gife I ſall few
The ordour of thair armes, it wer to tell heir;
The barris of beſt gold that I thame hail knew
It ſuld occupy ws all; thairfoir I end heir,
Refferring me to herraldis, to tell you the haill.
Off uthir ſcheildis, ſo ſchene,
Sum parte will I mene,
That wer on the tre grene
Worthy to waill.

XXII.

Secund ſyne, in a feild of ſilver certane *,
Off a kynd cullour the koddis I bend
With dowble treſſurs about, burely and bane,
And flour delycis ſo fair trewly to tend.
The tane and the tuthir of goulis full gane,
He bur quarterly, that nane mycht amend.
The armes of the DOWGLAS, thairof wes I fane,
Quhilk oft wes ſay with forſs, his fa till offend.
Off honorable anceſtry the armes of eld
Bur the Erle of MURRAY,
As ſad ſigne of affay,
His fell fais till affray,
In a fair feld.

* The coddis. *MS. margin.*

XXIII. Anc

XXIII.

Ane uthir, Erle of ORMOND, alſo he bure
The ſaid DowGLAs armes, with a difference.
And rycht ſo did the FERD*, quhair he furth fure;
Yaip thocht he yung was, to faynd his offence.
It ſemit that thay ſilver [war] for ſuth 1 aſſnre.
Thir four ſcheildis of price into preſence
Wer changit ſo chivelrouſs, that no creature
Of lokkis nor luikkis, mycht louſs worth a lence.
Syne ilk brench, and bew, bowit thame till:
And ilk ſcheild in that place   ♥
Thair tenent or man wace,
Or ellis thair all yace
At thair awin will.

XXIV.

Als hieſt in the crop four helmis full fair †,
And in thair tyime tall and tryd, trewly thay beir.
The pleſand *Powin* in a port, prowd to repare,
And als kepit ilk armes that I ſaid air.
The rowth wodroiſs wald that buſtouiſs bare,
Our growin gryſly and grym in effeir.
Mair awſnll in all thing ſall I nevare
Bayth to walk, and to ward, as withis in weir.
That drable felloun my ſpirit affrayit,
So ferdfull of fanteſy.
I durſt not kyth to copy
All uthir armes thairby,
Off renkis arrayit.

---

    * Lord Balveney. *MS. margin.*   † The Powin. *ib.*

XXV. Thair-

XXV.

Thairfoir of the faid tree I tell nocht the tend,
The birth, and the brenchis, that blomit fo bred.
Quhat fele armes on loft, lufly to lend,
Off lordingis in feir landis, gudly and glaid,
The faid Purfevand bur, quhair he away wend,
Off his garment fo gay, of ane he hede,
I leif thame blafound to be with herrauldis hend;
And I will to my matter as I air made.
And begyne, quhair I left, at lordingis dere,
The court of the Emprour,
How thay come in honour,
Thir fowlis of rigour
With a grit rere.

PART III.

P A R T　III.

A'R G U M E N T.

The poet returns to his fable. The temporal birds meet the fpiritual, and go to dinner, 1—v.—The Minftrels enter, vi.—Their hymn to the Virgin Mary, vii—ix.—The kinds of mufical inftruments, x.—The Jugler and his tricks, xi, xii.—The Irifh bard, and his fabulous fong, xiii.—His mad behaviour, and that of two fools, xiv—xvi.—After this fecond digreffion, the Council hear the owl's complaint, which is redreffed by Nature; but the owl's pride reduces her to her former uglinefs, xvii—xxv.—The owl's complaint, being the moral of the fable againft pride, xxv—xxvii.—Conclufion, xxviii.

I.

Than rerit thro membronis that montis fo he,
Furth borne bethleris bald in the bordouris;
Bufardis, and *Beld tyttes*, as it mycht be,
Soldwnris and fubject-men to thay Senyeoris.
The *Pitill* and the *Pipe gled* cryand *pewé*
Befoir thir prinoes ay paft, as pairt of purveyouris,
For thay culd cheires chikkynis, and purchafe poultré,
To cleik fra the commonis, as Kingis katouris
Syne hive honir and behald the harlry place.
Robene Reid-breft nocht ran,
Bot raid as a henfeman;
And the little we *Wran*
That wrechit dwerth was.

3

II.

Thair wes the herraldis fa the hobby but fable,
Stanchellis, *Steropis*, fcrycht to thair fterne lordis.
With alkin officiaris in erd, avenand and hable;
So mekle wes the multitude no mynd it remordis.   /
Thus affemblit thir feggis, firis fenyorable,
All that wer foulis of reif, quha richtly recordis,
For the Temporalite tretit in table.
The fterne Empriouris ftyle thus ftoutly reftord is.
The Paip, and the Patriarkis, the Prelattis, I wift,
Welcomit thame wyflie, but weir,
With haly farmondis feir,
Pardoun, and prayeir,   ' _
And blythly thame blift.

III.

The bliffit Paip in the place prayd thame ilk ane
To remane to the meit, at the midday ;
And thay grantit that gud, but gruching, to gane;
Than to ane wortheleth wane went thay thair way :
Paffit to a palice of price plefand allane,
Was erectit ryelly, ryke of array,
Pantit and apparalit prowdly in pane,
Sylit femely with filk, futhly to fay.
Braid burdis, and benkis, our beld with bancouris of gold,
Cled our with clene clathis,
Raylit full of richis,
The efreft wes the areffis
That ye fe fchold.

IV. All

                                                       /   ‑

IV.

All thus thay move to the meit: and the Marſchale *
Gart bring watter to weſche, of a well cleir:
That wes the *Falcone* ſo fair, frely but faile
Bad bernis burdis upbred, with a blyth chere.
The Paip paſt to his place, in his pontificale,
The athil Emprour annon nycht him neir.
Kings, and Patrearkis, kend with Cardynnallis all,
Addreſſit thame to that deſs, and Dukis ſo deir.
Biſchopis, Baronis, to the burd, and Marchonis of michtis;
Erlis of honoris,
Abbottis of ordoris,
Proveſtis and Prioris,
And many kene knychtis.

V.

Denis, and digneteis as are demit,
Scutiferis, and Sqyeris, and Bachelaris blyth:
I preſs nocht all to report; ye hard thame exprimit.
Bot all wer marchellit to meit mekly and myth:
Syne ſervit ſemely in ſale, forſuth as it ſemit,
With all curers of coſt that cukis coud kyth.
In fleſche tyme, quhen the fiſche wer away flemit,
Quha was Stewart bot the *Stork*, ſtalwart and ſtyth †:
Syne all the lentren but les, and the lang rede,
And als in the advent,
The *Soland* ſtewart was ſent;
For he coud fra the firmament
Fang the fiſche deid.

---

* Falcon-Marchell.　　　　† Stewarts. *MS. margin.*

2

VI. The

VI.

The *Boytour* callit was Cuke, that him weil kend *
In craftis of the kifchin, coftlyk of curi.
Mony fauouris fawce with fewans he fend,
And confectionnis of forfs that phefick furth furis.
Mony mair meitis, gife I fall mak end,
It neidis not to renew all thair naturis ;
Quhair fit ftaitis will fteir, thair ftyle till oftend,
Ye wait all welth and wirfchip daily induris.
Syne, at the middis of the meit, in come the Menftrallis †,
The *Mavifs* and the *Merle* fingis
Ofillis, and *Stirlingis* ;
The blyth *Lark* that begynis,
And the *Nychingallis.*

VII.

And thair notis in ane, gif I rycht nevin,
Were of Mary the myld ; the maner I wifs ;
" Hale temple of the trinité, crownit in hevin !
" Hale muder of our makar, and medecyn of mifs !
" Hale fritte and falve for the fynnis fevin !
" Hale but of e, barret and beld of our blifs !
" Hale granefull of grace that growis fo evin !
" Ferme our feid to the fet quhar thy-fone is.
" Haill lady of all ladies, lichteft of leine !
" Haill chalin of cheftité !
" Haill charbuncle of cherité !
" Haill ! Bliffit mot thou be
" For thy barne feine.

* Cuke, *MS. margin.*   † Menftralis, *ib.*

VIII.

" Haill bliffit throch the bodwird of blith angellis !
" Haill princes that expleitis all profetis pure !
" Haill blyther of the Bapteift, within thy bowellis,
" Of Elizabeth thy aunt, aganis nature !
" Haill fpritrous moft fpecifeit with the fprituallis !
" Haill ordanit or ordane, and ay to indure !
" Haill oure hope, and oure help, quhen that harme ailis !
" Haile altare of *Ena* in ane briture !
" Haile well of our weilfair ! We wait nocht of ellis ;
" Bot all comittis thé,
" Saull, and lyfe, Ladye :
" Now, for thy fruyte, mak us free
" Fra feindis that fellis.

IX.

" Fra thy gree to this ground lat thy grace glyde !
" As thow art grantare thairof, and the gevare ;
" Now fovrane quhair thow fittis, be thy fonis fyde,
" Send fum fuccor doun fone to the fynnare !
" The feind is our felloun fa, in thé we confyde,
" Thou moder of all mercye, and the menare.
" For ws wappit in wo in this warld wyde,
" To thy fone mak thy mane and thy makar.
" Now ladye luke to the lede that ye fo lele luifis,
" Thow fekir crone of *Salomon*,
" Thow worthy wand of *Aaron*,
" Thow joyis flece of *Jedron*,
" Us help the tahufis !"

X. All

X.

All thus our Ladye thai lofe, with lyking and lift,
Menftralis, and muficians, mo than I mene may.
The *Pfaltry*, the *Citholis*, the foft *atharift* *,
The *Cronde*, and the *monycordis*, the *gythornis* gay;
The *rote*, and the *recordour*, the *ribus*, the *rift*,
The *trump*, and the *taburn*, the *tympane* but tray;
The *lilt pype*, and the *lute*, the *cithill* and *fift*,
The *dulfate*, and the *dulfacordis*, the *fchalin* of affay;
The amyable *organis* ufit full oft;
Clarions loud knellis,
Portatibis, and *bellis*,
Cymbaellonis in the cellis,
That foundis fo oft.

XI.

Quhen thay had fangin, and faid, foftly a fchoure †;
And plaid as of paradyfs it a poynt ware;
In come japane the *Ja*, as a Jugloure,
With caftis, and with cantelis, a quynt caryare.
He gart thame fee, as it femyt, in famin houre,
Hunting at herdis, in holtis fo haire;
Soune failand on the fee fchippis of toure;
Bernis batalland on burd, brym as a bare;
He coud carye the coup of the kingis des,
Syne leve in the ftede
Bot a blak bunwede:
He coud of a henis hede
Mak a man mes.

* The kyndis of inftrumentis, *MS. margin.*   † The Sportaris, *ib.*

XII. He

XII.

He gart the Emproure trow, and trewlye behald,
That the *Corncraik*, the pundare at hand,
Had poyndit all his pris hors in a poynd fald,
Becaus thai eite of the corn in the kirkland.
He could wirk windaris, quhat way that he wald;
Mak a gray gus a gold garland,
A lang fpere of a bittill for a berne bald,
Noblis of nutfchellis, and filver of fand.
Thus jowkit with juxters the janglane *Ja.*
Fair ladyis in ringis,
Knychtis in caralyngis,
Bayth danfis and fingis;
It femyt as fa.

XIII.

Sa come the *Ruke* wi h a rerde, and a rane roch *,
A Bard out of *Irland* with *banochadee!*
Said, *gluntow guk dynydrach hala mifchty doch*;
Reke hir a rug of the roft, or fcho fall ryve thé.
Mifch makmory ach mach momitir moch loch;
Set her doun, gif her drink; quhat deill aylis ye?
O *Dermyn*, o *Donnal*, o *Dochardy droch*;
Thir ar the *Ireland* Kingis of the *Erchrye.*
O *Knewlyn*, o *Conoqubor*, o *Gregre M'Grane*;
The *Chenachy*, the *Clarfchach*,
The *Benefchene*, the *Ballach*,
The *Krekrye*, the *Corach*,
Scho kennis thame ilkane.

* The Ruke callit the Bard, *MS. margin.*

XIV. Monye

XIV.

Monye lefingis he maid; wat lat for no man
To fpeke quhill he fpokin had, fparet no thingis.
The Dene Rural, the *Ravin*, reprevit him than,
Bad him his lefingis leue befoir thai Lordingis.
The bard wes branewod, aud bitterlye coud ban,
" Thou corby meffinger," quoth he, " with forow now
    fingis ;
" Thow ifchit out of Noyis ark, and to the erd wan,
" Tareit as tratour and brocht na tadingis.
" I fall riwe the *Ravyn*, bayth guttis and gall.
Than the Dene Rurall worth rede,
Sall for fchame of the ftede.
The bard held a grit plede
In the hie hall.

XV.

In come twa flyrand Fulis with a fond fair *,
The *tuquheit*, and the gukkit *gowk*, and yede hiddie giddie;
Rwifchit bayth to the Bard, and ruggit his hare ;
Callit him thris thevis nek, to thraw in a widdie.
Than fylit him fra the foirtop to the fute thare.
The Bard fmaddit lyke a fmaik fmokit in a fmiddie :
Ran faft to the dur, and gaif a grit raure ;
Socht watter to wefch him thairout in ane ydy.
The Lordis leuch upoun loft, and lyking thai had,
That the Bard was fo let.
The Folis fend in the flet,
And monye mowis at mete
On the fluir maid.

      * The Fulis, *MS. margin.*

, XVI.

Syne for a figonale of frutt thai ftrave in the ftede;
The *tuqubeit* gird to the *gowk,* and gaif him a fall,
Raiff his taill fra his heid, with a rache pleid;
The *gowk* gat up agane in the grit hall,
Tuc the *tuqubeit* be the tope, and owirtirllit his heid,
Flang him flat in the fyre, fedderis and all.
He cryit, " Allace," with a rair, " revin is my reid!
" I am ungretiouflye gorrit bayth guttis and gall."
Yit he lopd fra ye low bycht in lyne.
Quhen thai had remyllis raucht,
Thai foirthocht that thai facht;
Kiffit fyne, and facht,
And fatt dcun fyne.

XVII.

All thus thir achilles in hall herlie remanit,
With all welthis at wifs, and wirfchip to waill:
The Pape beginnis to grace, as greablie ganit;
Wifch with thir wirehypis, and went to counfale.
The puir *Howlattis* appele complcitlie was planit,
His falt and foull forme, unfrelie but fale;
For the quhilk thir Loidis in lede nocht to lane it,
He befccht of focour, as fovrane in faile,
That thai wald pray Nature his prefent to renew;
Fcr it was hale his behefte,
At thair alleris iequefte,
Mycht dame Nature arefte
Of him for to rewe.

XVIII.

XVIII.

Than rewit thir ryallis of that rach man,
Bayth Spirituale and Temporale, that kennit the cas;
And, confiderand the caus, concludit in ane,
That thai wald NATURE befeke, of hir grit grace,
To difcend that faim hour as thair Sovrane,
At thair alleris inftance, in that ilk place.
The Pape and the Patriarkis, the Prelatis ilk ane,
Thus pray thai as penitent; and all that thair was.
Quhairthrow dame NATURE the traift difcendit that tyde,
At thair hale inftance;
Quham thai reffawe with reverance
And bowfum obeyfance,
As Goddes, and gyde.

XIX.

" It neides nocht," quoth NATURE, " to renew ocht
" Off your intent in this tyde, or for this to tell;
" I waitt your will, and quhat way ye wald that I wrocht
" To reafoun the *Houlate*, of faltis full fell.
" It fall be done at ye deme, drede ye rycht nocht:
" I confent in this cais to your counfell,
" Sen myfelf f.r your fake hidder hes focht.
" Ye fall be fpecialye fped, or I mair fpell.
" Now ilk foull of the firth a feddir fall ta,
" And len the *Houlat*, fen ye
" Of him hes pitie;
" And I fall gar thame famyn be
" To grow or I ga.

N 4   . XX. Thar

XX.

Than ilka foull o his facht a fether has tane,
And let the *Houlat* in hafte, hurthy but hone.
Dame Nature the nobilleft nychit in ane;
For fo ferm this fetheren, and dochly hes done;
Girt it ground, and grow gaylye and gane,
On the famin *Houlate*, femely and fone.
Than was the fchand of his fchaip, and his fchroud fchane
Off all coloure maift clere beldit abone;
The faireft foull of the firth, and hendeft of hewis;
So clene, and fo colourike,
That no bird was him lyke
Fro *Byron* to *Berwike*,
Under the bewis.

XXI.

Thus was *Houlat* in herd herdly at hicht,
Floure of all foulis, throw fetheris fo faire,
He lukit to his licame lemyt fo lycht,
So proper plefand of pient, proud to repaire.
He thocht maid on the mold makles of mycht,
As Sovrane him awin felf, throw beautie he baire,
Contitulate with the Pape our princis, I plicht;
Sy hielic he hyit him in Luciferis laire,
That all the foulis of the firth he defoulit fyne.
Thus lete he no man his pere;
Gif ony nygh wald him nere,
He bad thame rebaldis orere,
With a ruyne.

XXII. ' The

XXII.

‘ The Paip, and the Patriarkis, princis of prow,
‘ I am cum of thair blud, be coufingage knawin.
‘ So fair is my fetherein I haif no fallow ; ·
‘ My fchroud and my fchene were fchyre to be fchawin.
All birdis he rebawkit, that wald him nocht bow ;
In breth as a battell wrycht full of boft blawin,
With unlowable latis nocht till allow,
Thus vitiit he the Valantene thraly and thrawin.
That all the foulis with affent affemblit agane,
And plenyeit to Nature
Off this intollirable injure ;
How the *Houlat* him bure
So hé, and fo hautane.

XXIII.

So pompeous, impertinax, and reproviable,
In exceffis our arrogant thir birdis ilkane
Befocht Natur to ceifs that infufferable,
That with that Lady allyt lewch her allane.
“ My firft making,” quoth fcho, “ was unamendable,
“ Thocht I alterit, as ye all afkit in ane.
“ Yit fall I preif you to pleifs, for it is poffible.
Scho callit the *Howlat* in haift, that was fo hautane,
“ Thy pryd,” quoth the Princes, “ approchis our he,
“ Lyke Lucifer in eftait.
“ And for thow art fo elait,
“ As the Evangelift wrair,
“ Thow fall law be.

XXIV. “ The

XXIV.

" The rent, and the riches, that thow in rang,
" Wes of uthir menis all, and nocht of thryne awin ;
" Now ilk fowll his awin feddir fall againe fang ;
" And make the catyve of kynd, to thy felf knawin."
As fcho hes demyt thay haif done thraly in thrang.
Thairwith dame Natur hes to the hevin drawin :
Afcendit fone, in my ficht, with placence and fang.
And ilk foule tuke the flicht : and, fchortly to fchawin,
Held hame to thair hant, and to thair harbry,
Quhair thay wer wont to remane,
All thir gudly and gane :
And thair lenit allane
The *Howlate*, and I.

XXV.

Than this *Houlate* hideous of hair and of hyde,
Put firft fra poverty to prifs, and princes awin peir ;
Syne degradit fra grace, for his grit pryd,
Bannyt bittirly his birth belfully in beir.
He welterit, he wrythit, he wareit the tyd,
That he wes wrocht in this warld wofull in weir.
He criplit, he cryngit, he carefully cried,
He folpit, and forrowit, in fichingis feir.
He faid, " Allace I am loft, latheft of all,
" Byfym in bale beft ;
" I may be fimple heireft
" That pryd yit nevir left
" His feir, but a fall.

XXVI. " I

XXVI.

" I coud nocht won into welth wreth wayeft,
" I wes fo wantoun in will, my werdis ar wan;
" Thus for my hicht I am hurt and harmit in haift,
" Carfull and catife for craft that I can.
" Quhen I wes of hevit as heir all thill hieft,
" Fra rewll, reffon, and rycht redles I ran.
" Thairfoir I ly in the lymb, lympet the lathaift;
" Now mek your mirrour be me, all manner of man,
" Ye princis, prelettis of pryd for ponnyis and prow,
" That pullis the pure ay,
" Ye fall fing as I fay,
" ll your welth will away,
" Thus I werne yow.

XXVII.

" Think how bair thow wes borne, and bair ay will be,
" For ocht that fedis of thy felf, in ony fefon.
" Thy cud, thy claithis, thy coift, cumis nocht of thé,
" Bot of the frutt of the erd, and Gods fufron.
" Quhen ilka thing hes the awin, futhly we fe,
" Thy nakit corfs bot of clay and foule carion,
" Hatit, and hafles; quhairof art thow hé?
" We cum pure, we gang pure, bath King and Comon.
" Bot thow rewll thé richtoufs, thy crowne fall oureie."
Thus faid the *Houlate* on hicht.
Now God, for thy grit micht,
Set our faulis in ficht
Uff Sanctis fo feire!

XXVIII. Thus

XXVIII.

Thus for a *Dow* of DUNBAR drew I this dyte,
Dowit with a DOWGLAS; and baith were thay *Dowis*:
In the forreft foirfaid, frely perfyte,
Of *Terway*, tendir and tryd, quhofo treft trowis.
Wer my wit as my will, than fuld I weill wryte:
Bot gif lak in my leid, that nocht till all owis,
Ye wife, for your wirfchip, wryth me no wyte.
Now blyth ws the blift barne, that all berne bowis:
He len ws lyking and lyfe evirleftand!
In mirthfull moneth of May
In middis of *Murray*,
Thus in a tyme, be *Terrway*,
Hapnit HOLLAND.

EXPLICIT.

THE

THE

B L U D Y   S E R K,

A PIOUS FABLE.

MADE BY MR. ROBERT HENRYSON.

I.

This hundir yeir I have ben tald,
Thair was a worthy King;
Dukis, Erles, and Barronis bald,
He had at his bidding.
The Lord was anceane, and ald,
And fixty yeiris cowth ring.
He had a Dochter, fair to fald,
A lufty lady ying.

5   II. Of

II.

Off all fairheid fcho bur the flour;
And eik her fadris air :
Off lufty laitis, and hé honour;
Meik, botand debonair.
Scho wynnit in a bigly bour;
On fold wes none fo fair,
Princis luvit her peramour,
In Cuntreis our all quhair.

III.

Thair dwelt a lyt befyde the King
A fowll Gyane of ane ;
Stollin he he; the lady ying,
Away with hir is gane.
And keſt hir in his dungering,
Quhair licht fcho micht fe nane.
Hungir aud cauld, and grit thrifting,
Scho fand into hir wame.

IV.

He wes the louthlieſt on to luk
That on the grund mycht gang :
His nailis wes lyk ane hellis cruk,
Thairwith fyve quarteris lang.
Thair wes nane that he ourtuk,
In rycht or yit in wrang,
Bot all in fchondir he thame fchuk ;
The Gyane wes fo ſtrang.

V. He

V.

He held the lady day and nycht,
Within his deip dungeoun ;
He wald nocht gif of hir a ficht
For gold nor yit ranfoun.
Bot gife the King mycht get a Knycht,
To fecht with his perfoun,
To fecht with him, both day and nycht,
Quhill ane wer dungin doun.

VI.

The King gart feik bath fer and nere,
Beth be the te and land,
Off ony knycht gife he micht heir,
Wald fecht with that Gyand.
A worthy prince, that had no peir,
His tane the deid on hand,
For the luve of the lady cleir ;
And held full trew connand.

VII.

That prince come proudly to the toun,
Of that Gyane to heir ;
And faucht with him his awin perfoun,
And tuke him prefonier.
And keft him in his awin dungeoun,
Allane withouttin feir,
With hungir, cauld, and confufioun,
As full weill worthy weir.

VIII. Syne

VIII.

Syne brak the bour, had hame the bricht,
Unto hir fadir hé.
Sa evil wondit was the knycht,
That he behuvit to de.
Unlufum was his likame dicht;
His fark was all bludy;
In all the warld was nair a wicht
So petious for to fy.

IX.

The lady murnyt, and maid grit mone,
With all her mekle micht :
" I lufit nevir lufe, bot one,
" That dulfull now is dicht !
" God fen my lyfe wer fra me tone,
" Or I had fene yone ficht ;
" Or ellis in begging evir begone,
" Furth with yone curtafs knycht."

XII.

He faid, ' Fair lady now mone I
' De, treftly ye me trow.
' Tak ye my fark that is bludy,
' And hing it forrow you.
' Firft think on it, and fyne on me,
' Quhen men cumis yow to wow.'
The lady faid, " Be Mary fre,
" Thairto I mak a wow."

XI. " Qutun

XI.

Quhen that fcho lukit to the ferk,
Scho thocht on the perfoun :
And prayit for him with all her harte,
That lowfd her of bandoun,
Quhair fcho was wont to fit full merk
In that deip dungeoun.
And ever quhill fcho wes in quert
That wafs hir a leffoun.

XII.

So weill the lady luvit the Knycht
That no man wald fcho tak.
Sa fuld we do our God of micht *
That did all for us mak ;
Quhilk fullely to deid wes dicht,
For finfull manis faik.
Sa fuld we do, both day and nycht,
With prayaris to him mak.

XIII.

This Kingis lyk the Trinitie
Baith in hevin and heir.
The manis faule to the lady :
The Gyane to Lucefeir.
The Knycht to Chryft, that deit on tre,
And coft our fynnis deir :
The pit to hell, with panis fell ;
The fyn to the woweir.

* Moralitas, MS. *margie.*

XIV.

The Lady was woud, but ſcho ſaid nay,
With men that wald hir wed;
Sa ſuld we wryth all ſyn away,
That in our breiſt is bred.
I pray to Jeſu Chryſt verrey
For us his blud that bled,
To be our help on domyſday,
Quhair lawis ar ſtrontly led.

XV.

The ſaule is Goddis dochtir deir,
And eik his handewerk,
That was betraſit with Lucifeir,
Quha ſittis in hell full merk.
Borrowit with Chryſtis angell cleir,
Hend men will ye nocht herk?
For his luſe that bocht us ſa deir,
Think on the Bludy Serk!

Finis q. Mr. R. Henrici,

SIR GAWAN,

AND

SIR GALARON

OF

GALLOWAY;

A METRICAL ROMANCE.

O 2

SIR GAWAN,

AND

SIR GALARON

OF

GALLOWAY.

PART I.

ARGUMENT.

KING Arthur, and his queen Gaynour, or Genevra,
with her favorite knight Gawan, and others, go to
hunt near Carlile, *Stanza* I.—Her dreſs, II.—Gawan
and Gaynour alight. Arthur's hunting, III, IV, V.—
Darkneſs ariſes, VI.—The ghoſt of Gaynour's mother
appears, VII, VIII, IX, X.—Gawan queſtions it, and
its anſwer, XI, XII—Gawan brings Gaynour to it,
XIII.—The ghoſt adviſes charity, XIV.—And deſcribes
its miſery, XV.—Gaynour offers maſſes, XVI, XVII,
XVIII.—Enquires what moſt offended God ; anſwer,
pride, XIX.—What moſt pleaſes ; anſwer, humility
and charity, XX.—Gawan enquires concerning the

fate

fate of knights; and the ghoſt prophecies the fate of
Arthur and Gawan, xxi, xxii, xxiii, xxiv.—The
ghoſt takes its leave, xxv.—The day clears, and the
the court go to ſupper, xxvi.

All this is rather a digreſſive prologue, than part of the
tale, which properly begins at Part II.

I.

IN the tyme of ARTHUR an aunter bytyddc,
By the *Turnewathelan*, as the boke telles ;
Whan he to *Carlele* was comen, and conqueror kydd,
With Dukes, and Duſſiperes, that with the dere dwelles,
To hunt at the heides, that longe had ben hydde,
On a day thei hem deight to the depe delles ;
To fall of the femailes in foreſt, and frydde,
Fayre by the Firmyſthamis, in frithes, and felles.
Thus to wode arn thei went, the wlonkeſt in wedes,
Both the Kyng, and the Quene :
And all the douchti by dene ;
Sir GAWAYN, gayeſt on grene,
Dame GAYNOUR he ledes.

II.

Thus Schir GAWAYN, the gay, GAYNOUR he ledes,
In a gleterand gide, that glemed full gay,
With riche ribaynes reidſett, ho ſo right redes,
Rayled with rybees of rial aray.
Her hode of a herde huwe, that her hede hedes,
Of pillour, of palwerk, of perre to pay ;
Schurde in a ſhort cloke, that the rayne ſhedes,
Set over with ſaffres, ſothely to ſay,

With

With faffres, and fcladynes, fet by the fides.
Here fadel fette of that ilke,
Sande with fambutes of filke.
On a mule [whyte] as the mylke,
Gaili fhe glides.

III.

Al in gleterand golde gayly ho glides
The gates, with Sir GAWAYN, bi the grene welle.
And that barne, on his blonke, with the Quene bides ;
That borne was in borgoyne, by boke and by belle.
He ladde that ladye fo long by the lawe fides,
Under a lone they light lore by a felle.
And ARTHUR, with his Erles, erneftly rides,
To teche hem to her triftres, the trouthe for to tell.
To her triftres he hem taught, ho the trouth trowes,
Eche lord, withouten lette,
To an oke he hem fette ;
With bowe, and with barfelette,
Under the bowes.

IV.

Under the bowes thei bode, thes barnes fo bolde,
To byker at thes baraynes, in boukes fo bare.
There might hatheles in high herdes beholde ;
Herken huntyng in haft, in holtes fo hare.
Thei keft of here couples, in cliffes fo colde,
Conforte her kenettes, to hele hem of care;
Thei fel of the femayles ful thik folde:
With frefch houndes, and fele, thei folowen her fayre.
With gret queftes, and quelles,
Both in frith, and felles,
All the deeren in the delles
Thei durken, and dare.

V. Thei

V.

Thei durken the dere, in the dyme fkuwes,
That, for drede of the deth, droupis the do.
Thai werray the wylde fwyne, and worchen hem wo.
The huntis thei hallow, in hurftis and huwes;
And bluwe rechas; ryally thei ran to the ro;
They gef to no gamen, that on grounde gruwes:
The grete grendes, ih the grenes, fo gladly thei go,
So gladly thei gon, in greues fo grene.
The King blew rechas;
And folowed faft on the tras;
With many fergeant of mas,
That folas to fene.

VI.

With folas thei femble, the pruddeft in palle,
And fuwen to the foveraine, within fchaghes fchene.
Al but Schir GAWAYN, gayeft of all,
Belenes with Dame GAYNOUR in grenes fo grene.
Under a lorer ho was light, that lady fo fmall,
Of box, and of berber, bigged ful bene.
Faft byfore undre this ferly ccn fall,
And this mekel mervaile, that I fhal of mene.
Now wol I of this mervaile mene, if I mote.
The day wex als dirke,
As hit were mydnight myrke;
Thereof the King was irke;
And-light on his fote.

VII. Thus

VII.

Thus to fote ar thei faren, thes frekes unfayn,
And fleen fro the foreſt to the fewe felles ;
For the fuetand fuawe fuartly hem fuelles.
There come a Lede of the Lawe, in londe is not to layne,
And glides to Schir GAWAYNE, the gates to gayne;
Yauland, and yomerand, with many loude yelles,
Hit yaules, hit yamers, with waymyng wete,
And feid, with fiking fare,
" I ban the body me bare !
" Alas now kindeles my care !
" I gloppe, and I grete."

VIII.

Then gloppenet, and grete, GAYNOUR the gay,
And feid to Sir GAWEN, " What is thi good rede ?"
" Hit ar the clippes of the fon, I herd a clerk fay."
And thus he confortes the Quene for his knighthede.
" Schir CADOR, Schir CLEGOR, Schir COSTANDYNE,
    " Schir CAY,
" Thes knyghtes arn curtays, by croſſe, and by crede,
" That thus oonly have me laft on my deythe day,
" With the griſſeliſt Gooſt, that ever herd I grede."
' Of the gooſt,' quod the grome, ' greve you no mare.
' For I ſhal ſpeke with the ſprete,
' And of the wayes I ſhal wete,
' What may the bales bete,
' Of the bodi bare.'

IX. Bare

IX.

Bare was the body, and blak to the bone,
Al biclagged in clay, uncomly cladde.
Hit waried hit wayment, as a woman ;
But on hide, ne on huwe, no heling hit hadde.
Hit stemered ; hit stonayde ; hit stode as a stone :
Hit marred ; hit memered ; hit mused for madde.
Agayn the grisly Goost Schir GAWAYN is gone ;
He ra\ked out at a res, for was never drad ;
Drad was he never, ho so right redes.
On the chef of the clolle,
A pade pik on the polle ;
With eighen holked full holle,
That gloed as the gledes.

X.

Al glowed as a glede, the golle there ho glides,
Umbeclipped him, with a cloude of cleyng unclere,
Skeled with serpentes, all aboute the sides ;
To tell the todes theron my tongue wer full tere.
The barne braides out the bronde, and the body bides,
Therefor the chevalrous knight changed no chere.
The houndes highen to the wode, and her hede hides,
For the grisly goost made a grym bere :
The grete grenndes wer agast of the grym bere,
The birdes in the bowes,
That on the goost glowes,
Thai stryke in the skowes,
That hatheles may here.

XI. Ha-

XI.

Hathelefe might here fo fer into halle,
How chateted the cholle, the chalous on the chyne,
Then comred the Knight, on Crift can he calle,
' As thou was crucifized on croys, to clanfe us of fyn,
' That thou fei me the fothe, whether thou fhalle,
' And whi thou walkeft thes wayes the wodes within?
—" I was of figure, and face, faireft of alle;
" Criftened, and knowen, with King in my kyne;
" I have King in my kyn knowen for kene.
" God has me geven of his grace,
" To dre my paynes in this place.
" I am comen, in this cace,
" To fpeke with your Quene.

XII.

" Quene was I fomwile, brighter of browes
" Then BERELL, or BRANGWAYN, thes burdes fo bolde;
" Of al gamen, or gle, that on grounde growes;
" Gretter than Dame GAYNOUR, of garfon, and golde, ·
" Of palacis, of parkis, of pondis, of plowes;
" Ot townis, of touris, of treffour untolde;
" Of caftellis, of contreyes, of craggis, of clowes.
" Now am I caught out of kide to cares fo colde;
" Into care am I caught, and couched in clay.
" Se, Schir curtays Knight,
" How dolfulle deth has me dight,
" Lete me onys have a fight
· " Of GAYNOUR the gay."

XIII. After

XIII.

After GAYNOUR, the gay, Schir GAWAYN is gon,
And to the body he hes brought, and to the burde bright,
" Welcome WAYNOUR I wis worthi in won
" Lo how delful deth has thi Dame dight!
" I was radder of rode then rose in the ron;
" My lever, as the lelé, lonched on hight.
" Now am I a gracelefs gaft; and grifly I gron.
" With LUCYFER, in a lake, logh am I light.
" Take truly tent tight nowe by me;
" For al thi frefch favoure
" Mufe on my mirrour.
" For King, and Emperour,
" Thus fhal ye be.

XIV.

" Thus dight wil you dight, thare you not doute;
" Thereon hertly take hede, while th u ar here.
" Whan thou art richeft araied, and richeft in thi route,
" Have pité on the poer, thou art of powér.
" Barnis, and burdis, that ben ye aboute,
" When thi body is bamed, and brought on a ber,
" Then lite wyn the light, that now will the loute;
" For then he helpes nothing, but holy praier.
" The praier of poer may purchas thé pes,
" Of that thou yeves at the yete,
" When thou art fet in thi fete,
" With all merthis at mete,
" And dayntes on des.

5   XV. " With

XV.

" With riche dayntes on des thi drotes art dight;
" And I in danger, and doel, in dongon I dwelle,
" Naxté, and nedeful, naked on night;
" Ther folo me a ferde of fendes of helle.
" They hurle me unhendeley, thai harme me in hight;
" In bras, and in brymfton, I bren as a belle.
" Was never wrought in this world a wofuller wight.
" Hit were ful tore any tonge my torment to telle.
" Nowe wil I of my torment tel, or I go.
" Thenk hertly on this,
" Fonde to mende thi mys.
" Thou art warned y wys.
" Bewar be my wo !"

XVI.

' Wo is me for thi wo !' quod WAYNOUR, ' y wys.'
' But one thing wold I wite, if thi wil ware.
' If anyes matens, or mas, might mende thi mys,
' Or eny meble on molde; my merthe were the mare.
' If bedis of bifhoppis might bring the to blifle;
' Or coventes in cloiftre might kere the of care.
' If thou be my moder, grete wonder hit is
' That al thi burly body is brought to be fo bare.'
" —I bare the of my body; what bote is hit I layn?
" I brak a folempne vow,
' And no man wift hit, but thowe;
" By that token thou trowe
" That fothely I fayn,"

XVII. ' Say

XVII.

‘ Say fothely what may ye favert, y wys ;
‘ And I fhal make fere men to finge for thi fake.
‘ But the baleful beftis that on thi body is !
‘ Al bledes my ble, thi bonos arne fo blake.’
“ That is luf paramour, liftis, and delites,
“ That has me light, and laft logh in a lake.
“ Al the welth of the world, that awey wites,
“ With the wilde wermis that worche me wrake.
“ Wrake thei me worchen, WAYNOUR, I wyf !
“ Were thritty trentales don,
“ Bytwene under and non,
“ Mi foule focoured with fon,
“ And brought to the blys.”

XVIII.

‘ To blille bring thé the barne, that bought thé on rode !
‘ That was crucifiged on croys, and crowned with thorne.
‘ As you was criftened, and crefomed, with candle and code,
‘ Folowed in fouteftone, on frely byforne.
‘ MARY the mighti, myldelt of mode,
‘ Of whom the blisful barne in *Bedlem* was borne,
‘ Leve me grace that I may grete ye with gode ;
‘ And mynge ye with matens, and malles on morne.
“ To mende us with malles grete myfter hit were.
“ For him, that reft on the rode,
“ Gyf faft of thi goode
“ To folk that failen the fode ;
“ While thou art here.

4

XIX.

‘ Here hertly my honde, thes heftes to holde,
‘ With a myllion of maffes to make the mynyng.
‘ A !’ quod WAYNOUR, ‘ I wys yit weten I wolde,
‘ What wrathed God moft at thi weting ?’
—‘‘ Pride, with the appurtenance ; as prophetes [hokle]
‘‘ Bifore the peple, apt in her preching.
‘‘ Hit heres bowes bitter, therof be thou bolde,
‘‘ That mak barnes fo bly to breke hjs bidding ;
‘‘ But ho his bidding brek, bare thei ben of blys.
‘‘ But thei be falved of that fare,
‘‘ Er thei hepen fare,
‘‘ They mon weten of care,
‘‘ WAYNOUR, I wys.’’

XX.

‘ Wyffe me.’ quod WAYNOUR, ‘ fom wey, if thou woft,
‘ What bedis might me beft to the bliffe bring.’
—‘‘ Mekeneffe, and mercy, thes arn the mooft.
‘‘ And fithen have pité on the poer : that plefes heven king.
‘‘ Sithen charité is chef, and then is chafte ;
‘‘ And then almeffe dede cure al thing.
‘‘ Thes arn the graceful giftes of the Holy Gofte,
‘‘ That enfpires iche fprete, withoute fpeling.
‘‘ Of this fpiritual thing fpute thou no mare.
‘‘ Als thou art Quene in thi quert,
‘‘ Hol l thes wordes in hert.
‘‘ Thou fhal leve but a ftert :
‘‘ Hethen fhal thou fare.’’

XXI. ‘ How

XXI.

‘ How fhal we fare,’ quod the Freke, ‘ that fonden to fight,
And thus defoulen the folke, on fele king londes,
‘ And riches over reymes, withoutten eny right,
‘ Wynnen worfhipp in werre, though wightneffe of hondes?’
—“ Your King is to covetous, I warne thé, Schir Knight.
“ May no man ftry him with ftrength, while his whele
     “ ftondes.
“ Whan he is in his magefté, mooft in his might,
“ He fhal light ful lowe on the fe fondes.
“ And this chivalrous knight chef fhal thorgh chaunce
“ Falfely fordone in fight,
“ With a wonderful wight,
“ Shal make lordes to light ;
“ Take witneffe by *Fraunce.*

XXII.

“ *Fraunce* hath haf the frely with your fight wonnen ;
“ *Freol,* and his folke, fey ar they leved.
“ *Bretayne,* and *Burgoyne,* al to you bowen,
“ And all the Duffiperes of *Fraunce* with your dyn deved.
“ *Gyan* may grete the werre was bigonnen ;
“ There ar no lordes on lyve in that londe leved.
“ Yet fhal the riche remayns with one be overronen,
“ And with the Rounde Table the rentes be reved.
“ Thus fhal a Tyber untrue tymber with tene.
“ Gete the Schir GAWAYN,
“ Turne the to *Tufkayn,*
“ For ye fhal lefe *Bretayn*
“ Wlth a King kene.

XXIII. “ This

XXIII.

" This Knight fhal be clanly enclofed with a crowne;
" And at *Carlele* fhal that comly be crowned as King.
" A fege fhal he feche with a feffioun,
" That myche baret, and bale, to *Bretayn* fhal bring.
" Hit fhal in *Tufkayn* be tolde of the trefoun,
" And ye fhullen turne ajen for the tything.
" Ther fhal the Rounde Table lefe the renoune
" Befide *Ramfey* ful rad, at a riding :
" In *Dorfetfhire* fhal dy the doughteft of alle.
" Gete the Schir GAWAYN,
" The boldeft of *Bretayne*;
" In a flake thou fhal be flayne.
" Sich ferlyes fhul falle !

XXIV.

" Such ferlies fhul fal, withoute eny fable,
" Uppon *Cornewayle* cooft, with a knight kene,
" Schir ARTHUR the honeft, avenant, and able,
" He fhal be wounded, I wys, woyeley I wene.
" And al the rial rowte of the Rounde Table,
" Thei fhullen dye on a day, the doughty bydene.
" Supprifet with a furget, he beris hit in fable,
" With a fauter engreled, of filver full fhene ;
" He beris hit of fable, fothely to fay.
" In riche ARTHURES halle,
" The barne playes at the balle,
" That ontray fhal you alle,
" Delfully that day.

Vol. III. P XXV. " Have

XXV.

" Have gode day GAYNOUR, and GAWAYN the gode;
" I have no lenger to me tidinges [to] telle.
" I mote walke on my wey, thorgh this wilde wode:
" In my wonyng-ftid, in wo for to dwelle.
" Fore him, that right wifly rofe, and reft on the rode,
" Thenke on the danger, that I yn dwell.
" Fede folke, for my fake, that failen the fode;
" And menge me with matens, and maffes in melle.
" Maffes arn medecynes, to us that bale bides.
" Us thenke a maffe as fwete,
" As eny fpice that ever ye yete."
——With a grifly grete,
   The gofte awey glides.

XXVI.

With a grifly grete the gooft awey glides;
And goes, with gronyng fore, thorgh the greves grene,
The wyndes, the weders, the welken unhides;
Then unclofed the cloudes, the fon con fhene.
The King his bugle has blowen, and on the bent bides,
His fare folke in the frith thei flokken bydene.
And al the rial route to the Quene rides.
She fayis hem the felcouthes, that thai hadde yfeene:
The wife of the weder forwondred they were.
Prince proudeft in palle,
Dame GAYNOUR, and alle,
Went to *Rondoles halle*,
To the fuppere.

                     PART

PART   II.

ARGUMENT.

Arthur being at fupper a lady leads in a knight errant,
who afterwards proves to be Sir Galaron, i.—Arthur
promifes juftice, ii.—Drefs of the lady and knight, iii,
iv, v.—Arthur enquires, and Galaron declares his
name, and claims his lands conquered by Arthur,
vi, vii.—The knight led to a pavilion to reft all night,
viii, ix.—Gawan offers to fight, and the lifts appointed, x, xi.—Galaron leaves his lady in Gaynour's
care ; and the fight begins, xii, xiii.—The combat
defcribed, Gawan's fteed Griffelt flain, xiv, xv, xvi,
xvii.—Fight on foot, xviii.—Both wounded, xix.
—Gaynour weeps for Gawan's danger, xx.—Galaron
is worfted, and his lady intercedes with Gaynour, xxi,
xxii.—And Gaynour with Arthur, xxiii.—Galaron
yields, and Arthur commands peace, xxiv, xxv.—
Arthur gives Galaron lands in Wales, xxvi,—and Gaynour gives Galaron his lands, xxvii.—Sir Galaron
married, and made a knight of the Round Table,
xxviii.—Gaynour orders maffes for her mother, xxix.

P 2   I. THE

I.

THE King to fouper is fet, ferved in halle,
Under a filler of filke, dayntly dight;
With al worfhipp, and wele, mewith the walle ;
Briddes branden, and brad, in bankers bright.
There come in a foteler, with a fymballe,
A lady, lufsom of lete, ledand a knight
Ho raykes up in a res bifor the rialle ;
And halfed Schir ARTHUR, hendly on hight.
Ho faid to the foverayne, wlonkeft in wede,
‘ Mon makeles of might,
‘ Here comes an Errant Knight.
‘ Do him refon, and right,
‘ For thi manhede.’

II.

Mon in the mantell, that fittis at thi mete,
In pal pured to pay, prodly pight.
The taffes were of topas, that were thereto tight.
He gliffed up with his eighen, that grey wer, and grete;
With his beveren berde, on that burde bright.
He was the foverayneft of al fitting in fete,
That ever fegge had fen with his eghe fight.
King crowned in kith talk hir tille ;
‘ Welcome worthely wight ;
‘ He fhal have refon, and right.
‘ Whelen is the comli knight .
‘ If hit be thi wille ?’

III. Ho

III.

Ho was the worthieſt wight, that eny wede wolde.
Here gide was glorious, and gay, of a greſſe grene ;
Here belte was of blunket, with birdes ful bolde,
Branded with brende golde, and bokeled ful bene.
Her fax in fyne furre was fretted in folde,
Contrefeled and kelle coloured full clene,
With a crowne craſtly, al of clene golde :
Here kercheves were curiouſe with many proude pene.
Her perre was prayſed, with priſe men of might.
Bright birdes, and bolde,
Had inore to beholde
Of that frely to folde,
And on the hende knight.

IV.

The Knight in his colours was armed ful clene,
With his comly creſt, clere to beholde.
His brene, and his baſnet, burneſhed ful bene.
With a brandur abought, al of brende golde.
His mayles were mylke white, many hit fene.
His horſe trapped of that ilke, as true men me tolde.
His ſhelde on his ſhulder, of ſilver ſo ſhene,
With bere hedes of brake, browed ful bolde.
His horſe in fyne ſaudel was trapped to the hele.
And, in his cheveron biforne,
Stode as an unicorne,
Als ſharp as a thorne,
An anlas of ſtele.

P 3   V. In

V.

In ſtele he was ſtuffed, that ſtourne uppon ſtede,
Al of ſternes of golde ; his pencell diſplaied ;
His gloves, his gameſons, glowed as a glede ;
With graynes of reve that graied ben gay.
And his ſchene ſchynbandes, that ſharp wer to ſhrede ;
His polemous with pelicocus were poudred to pay.
With a launce on loft that lovely con lede.
A freke, on a freſon, him folowed in ſay :
The freſon was afered for drede of that fare.
For he was ſelden wonte to ſe
The tablet fluré.
Siche gamen ne gle
Sagh he never are.

VI.

ARTHUR aſked on hight, herand hem alle,
" What woldes thou, wee, if hit be thi wille ?
" Tell me what thou ſeches, and whether thou ſhalle ?
" And whi thou ſturne on thi ſlede, ſtondes ſo ſtille ?"
He wayned up his viſer fro his ventalle ;
With a knightly contenaunce he carpes him tille.
' Whether thou Cayſer, or King, her I thé becalle
' Fore to finde me a freke, to fight with my fille.
' Fighting to fraiſt, I fonded fro home.'
Then ſeid the King uppon hight,
" If thou be curteys Knight,
" Late lenge al nyght,
" And tel me thi nome."

VII.

‘ Mi name is Schir GALARON, withouten eny gile;
‘ The greteſt of *Galwey*, of grenes and grylles,
‘ Of *Connok*, of *Conyngham*, and alſo *Kyle*;
‘ Of *Lomond*, of *Loſex*, of *Lothan* hilles.
‘ Thou has wonen hem in werre with a wrange wille;
‘ And geven hem to Schir GAWAYN, that my hert grylles.
‘ But he ſhal wring his honde, and warry the wyle,
‘ Er he weld hem, y wis, agayn myn umwylles.
‘ Bi al the welth of the worlde, he ſhal hem never welde,
‘ While I the hede may bere;
‘ But if he wyn hem in were,
‘ With a ſhelde, and a ſpere,
‘ On a faire felde.

VIII.

‘ I wol fight on a felde, thereto I make feith,
‘ With any freke uppon folde, that frely is borne.
‘ To leſe ſuche a lordſhipp me wold thenke laith;
‘ And iche lede opon lyve wold lagh me to ſcorne.
—‘‘ We ar in the wode went, to walke on oure waith,
‘‘ To hunt at the hertes, with honde, and with horne;
‘‘ We ar in our gamen, we have no gome-graithe.
‘‘ But yet thou ſhalt be mached be mydday to morne.
‘‘ Forthi I rede the thenke reſt al night.’’
GAWAYN, gratheſt of all,
Ledes him oute of the halle,
Into a pavilon of pall,
That prodly was pight.

IX. Pight

IX.

Pight was prodly, with purpour and palle ;
Birdes branden above, in breud gold bright;
Ruwith was a chapell, a chamboúr, a halle ;
A chymné with charcole, to chaufe the Knight.
His ftede was ftabled, and led to the ftalle,
Hay hertely he had in haches on hight.
Sithen thei braide up a borde, and clothes thei calle;
Sanapé, and faler, femly to fight,
Torches, and brochetes, and ftondardes bitwene.
Thus thei ferved that Knight,
And his worthely wight,
With riche dayntés dight,
In filver fo fhene.

X.

In filver fo femely were ferved of the beft,
With vernage, in veres, and cuppes ful clene.
And thus Schir GAWAYN, the good, glades hor geft,
With riche dayntees, endored in difshes bydene.
Whan the riall renke was gon to his reft,
The King to counfaile has called his Knightes fo kene.
" Loke now lordis our lofe be not loft,
" Ho fhal encountre with the Knight keft you bitwene.
Then faid GAWAYN the goode, ' Shal hit not greve,
' Here my honde I you hight,
' I woll fight with the Knight,
' In defence of my right,
' Lorde, by your leve

5   XI. " I

XI.

" I leve wel," quod the King, " thi latis ar light;
" But I nolde, for no lordefhippe, fe thi life lorne."
' Let go,' quod Schir GAWAYN, 'God ftoni with the right;
' If he fkape fkathelefe hit were a foule fkorne.'
In the daying of the day, the doughti were dight ;
And heren matens and maffe erly on morne.
By that on Plutonland a palais was pight,
Were never freke opon folde had foughten biforne.
Thei fetten liftes by lyne on the logh lande.
Thre foppes de mayn
Thei brought to Schir GAWAYN,
For to confort his brayn ;
The King gared commaunde.

XII.

The King commaunded KRUDELY, the Erlis fon of *Kent*,
Curtayfley in this cafe take kepe to the Knight.
With riche dayntees, or day, he dynes in his tente;
After bufk him in a brene that burnefhed was bright.
Sithen to WAYNOUR wifly he went;
He laft in here warde his worthy wight.
After ARTHER in high hour horfes thei hent,
And at the liftes on the lande lordely don light,
Both thes two barnes, baldeft of blode,
The king chaier is fet,
Quene on a chacelet.
Many galiard gret
For GAWAYN the gode,

XIII. GAWAYN

XIII.

Gawayn and Galeron gurden her ſtedes,
Al in gleterand golde gay was here gere.
The lordes by lyne hom to liſt ledes,
With many ſerjant of mace, as was the manere.
Th- barnes broched the blonke that the ſide bledis.
Ayther freke opon folde has faſtned his ſpere.
Shaftes in ſhide woðe thei ſhindre in ſhedes;
So joliîé thes gentil juſted on were.
Shaftes thei ſhindr in ſheldes ſo ſhene:
And ſithen, with brondes bright,
Riche mayles thei right.
There encontres the Knight
With Gawyn on grene.

XIV.

Gawyn was gaily grathed in grene,
With his griffons of gold, engreled full gay,
Trifeled with tranes, and true loves bitwene,
On a ſtargand ſtede that ſtrikes on ſtray.
That other in his turnaying he talkes in tene,
‘ Why drawes thou the on dregh, and mak ſiche deray ?
He ſwapped him then at the ſwayne, with a ſwerde kene:
That greved Schir Gawayn, to his deth day.
The dyntes of that doughty were doutwis bydene.
Fitté mayles, and mo,
The ſwerde ſwapt in two,
The canel bone alſo ;
And clef his ſhelde ſhene.

XV. He

XV.

He clef thorgh the cautel, that covered the Knight,
Thorgh the fhinand fhelde, a fhaftmon, and mare ;
And then the lady loude lowe uppon hight,
And GAWAYN greches therwith, and greved ful fare.
‘ I fhal rewarde the thi route, if I con rede right.’
He folowed in on the freke, with a frefch fare,
Thorgh blafon, and brene, that burnefhed were bright,
With a burlich brande, thorgh him he bare.
The bronde was bludy, that burnefhed was bright.
Then gloppened that gay :
Hit was no ferly, in fay.
The flurne flrik on flray
In fliropis flright.

XVI.

Streyte on his fleroppis floutely he flrikes,
And waynes at chir WAWAYN als he were wode.
Then his leman on lowde fkirles, and fkrikes,
When that burly barne blenket on blode.
Lordis and ladies of that laike likes ;
And thonked God fele fithe for GAWAYN the gode.
With a fwap of a fwerde that fwathel him fwykes,
He flreke of the flede-hede, flreite there he flode.
The faire fole fondred, and fel to the grounde.
GAWAYN gloppened in hert,
Of he were hafty and fmert.
Out of flerops he flerr,
For *Griffelt* the goode.

XVII. ‘ *Griffelt*, ’

XVII.

‘ *Griffelt*,’ quod GAWAYN, ‘ gon is, God wote !
‘ He was the burlokeſt blonke, that ever bote brede.
‘ By him, that in *Bedeleem* was borne ever to ben our bote,
‘ I ſhall venge thé to day, if I con right rede.
‘ Go feeche me my Freſon, faireſt on fote,
‘ He may ſtonde thé in ſtoure in as mekle ſtede.
‘ No more for the faire fole, then for a riſh rote,
‘ But for doel of the dombe beſt, that thus ſhuld be dede,
‘ I mourne for no montur, for I may gete mare.’
Als he ſtode by his ſiede,
That was ſo goode at neede.
Ner GAWAYN wax wede,
So ſiked he fare.

XVIII.

Thus wepus for wo WAWAYN the wight ;
And wenys him to q ryte that wonded is fare.
That other drogh him on dreght, for drede of the knight,
And holdely broched his blonk on the bent bare.
Thus may thei dryve forth the day, to the derk night:
The ſun was paſſed, by that, mydday, and mare.
Within the liſes the lede lordly don light ;
Touard the barne, with his bronde, he buſked him yare.
To bataile they bowe with brondes ſo bright.
Shene ſheldes wer ſhred ;
Bright brenes by bled.
Many doughti were adred :
So ferſely thei fight.

XIX. Thus

XIX.

Thus thei feght on fote, on that fair felde,
As frefsh as a lyon, that fautes the ll e.
Wilelé thes wight men thair wepenes they welde,
He * bronched him † yn, with his bronde, under the brode
    fhelde.
Thorgh the waaft of the body, and wonded him ille:
The fverde ftent for no ftuf hit was fo wel fleleiL
That other ftartis on bak, and ftandis fton ftille;
Though he were ftcnayd, that ftonde he ftrik ful fare.
He gurdes to Sehir GAWAYN,
Thorgh ventaile, and pefayn.
He wanted noght to be flayn
The brede of an hare.

XX.

Hardely then thes hatbeleffe on helmes they hewe,
Thei beten down beriles, and bourdures bright;
Shildes on fhildres, that fhene were to fhewe,
Fretted were in fyne golde, thei failen in fight.
Stones of fral they ftrenkel, and ftrewe;
Stithe ftapeles of ftele they ftrike don ftight.
Barnes bannen the tyme the bargan was brewe,
The doughti with dyntes fo delfully were dight.
Then gretes GAYNOUR, with bothe her gray eae;
For tho doughti that fight,
Were manly mached of might,
Withoute refon, or right,
As al men fene.

       * Gawan.   † Galaron.

XXI. Thus

XXI.

Thus gretis GAYNOUR, with bothe her gray yene,
For gref of Schir GAWAYN grifly was wounded.
The Knight of corage was cruel and kene ;
And with a ftéle brande, that fturneft ftonded,
Al the coft of the Knyght, he carfe downe clene ;
Thorgh the riche mailes, that ronke were, and rounde,
With a teneful touche he taght him in tene,
He gurdes Schir GALERON groveling on gronde.
Grifly on gronde he groned on grene.
Als wounded as he was,
Sone buredely he ras,
And falowed faft on his tras,
With a fwerde kene.

XXII.

Kenely that cruel kenered on hight,
And with a fcas of care in cautil he ftrik,
And waynes at Schir WAWYN that worthely wight,
But him lymped the worfe ; and that me wel lik.
He atteled with a flenk haf flayn him in flight ;
The fwerd fwapped on his fwange, and on the mayle flik.
And GAWAYN bi the coler keppis the knight ;
Then his leman on loft fkrilles and fkrik.
Ho gret on GAYNOUR, with gronyng grylle,
‘ Lady, makeles of might,
‘ Haf mercy on yondre Knight,
‘ That is fo delfull d'ght,
‘ If hit be thi wille.’

XXIII. Wifly

XXIII.

Wifly Dame Waynour to the King went;
Ho caught of her coronall ; and kneled him tille.
" As thou art joy roial, richeft of rent,
" And I thi wife, wedded at thi owne wille,
" Thes barnes in the bataile fo blede on the bent,
" They arn wery, I wis ; and wonded full ille.
" Thorgh her fhene fheldes her fhuldres ar fhent,
" The grones of Schir Gawayn dos my hert grille.
" The grones of Schir Gawayn greven me fare.
" Woldeft thou Leve Lorde
" Make thes Knights accorde,
" Hit were a grete conforde,
" For all that ther ware."

XXIV.

Then fpak Schir Galeron to Gawayn the good;
' I wende never wee, in this world, had ben half fo wight;'
' Her I make the releyfe, renke, by the rode ;
' And by rial reyfon relefe the my right.
' And fithen make the moraden with a mylde mode,
' As man of medlert makeles of might.'
He talkes touard the King, on hie ther he ftode,
And bede that burly his bronde, that burnesfhed was
        bright.
' Of rentes and richeffe I make the releyfe,
Downe kneled the Knight,
And carped wordes on hight ;
The King ftode upright,
And commaunded pes.

        XXV. The

XXV.

The King commaunded pes, and cried on hight;
And GAWAYN was goodly, and laft for his fake,
Then lordes to lifles they lopen ful light,
Schir GWAYN FITZ GRIAN, and ARRAK FITZ LAKE;
Schir DRURELAT, and MOYLARD, that moſt wer of
　　might,
Both thes travayled men they truly up take.
Unneth might tho ſturne ſtonde upright,
What for buffetes and blode her blees wex blake.
Her blees were brofed for beting of brondes.
Withouten more lettyng,
Dight was here faghtlyng,
Bifore the comly King,
Thei held up her hondes.

XXVI.

" Here I gif Schir GAWAYN; with gerfon, and golde,
" All the *Glamorgan* lande, with greves fo grene;
" The worſhip of *Wales*, at wil and at wolde;
" With Griffones caftelles, curnelled full clene.
" Eke *Ulſturhalle*, to hafe, and to holde;
" *Wayford*, and *Waterforde*, in Wales I wene.
" Two barounees in *Bretayne*, with burghes fo bolde,
" That arn batailed abought, and bigged ful bene.
" I fhall dight the a Duke, and dubbe the with honde.
" Withy thou faghtil with the Knight,
" That is fo hardi and wight,
" And relefe him his right,
" And graunte him his londe."

XXVII.

XXVII.

‘ Here I gif Schir GALERON,’ quod GAYNOUR, ‘ with-
‘ outen any gile,
‘ Al the londis, and the lithis, fro laver to layr e;
‘ Connok, and Carlele, Conyngham, and Kile ;
‘ Yet if he of chevalry, and chalange hair in for air;
‘ The Loth, the Lemok, the Loynak, the Lile,
‘ With frithis, and foreſtis, and foſſis fo faire :
‘ Under your lordeſhip to lenge hevenwhile,
‘ And to the Rounde Table to make repayre.
‘ I ſhall refeff him in felde, in foreſt to far e
Bothe the King, and the Quene,
Andal the doughti bydene,
Thorgh the greves fo grene,
Carlele thei care.

XXVIII.

The King to Carlele is comen, with Knight fo kene ;
And al the Rounde Table on rial aray.
The wees, that weren wounded fo wothely, I wene,
Surgenes fone faned, fothely to fay.
Bothe confortes the Knight, the King and the Quene.
Thei were dubbed Dukes both on a day.
There he wedded his wife, wlonkeſt, I wene,
With giftes, and garſons, Schir GALERON the gay.
Thus that hathel in high withholdes that hende.
Whan he was faned fonde,
Thei made Schir GALERON that ſtonde,
A Knight of the Table Ronde,
To his lyves ende.

XXIX.

WAYNOUR gared wifely write in the weft,
To all the religious, to rede and to finge ;
Preftes with proceffion to pray were preft,
With a mylion of maffes, to make the mynynge.
Boke-lered men, bisfhops the beft,
Thorgh al *Bretayne* befely the burde gared rynge.
This ferely bifelle in *Englond* foreft,
Under a holte fo hore, at a huntynge.
Suche a huntyng in haaft is noght to behide :
Thus to foreft they fore,
Thes fterne Knights on ftore.
In the tyme of ARTHORE
This aunter betide.

GLOSSARY.

G L O S S A R Y.

*** THE frequent alliterations ufed in thefe poems have often conftrained the authors to ufe words in a moft oblique fenfe, and fometimes with no fenfe at all; hence many words are inferted with a point of interrogation, tho the ufual meaning be well known.

A

Abaid, *delay.*
Abulyement, *habit, drefs.*
Achil, *high?* III. 158, 160, athil, 176, achilles, 182, *and fee* hathils.
Adjutorie, *aid.*
Adrad, *afraid.*
Age, *edge.*
Aiken, *oaken.*
Air, *heir, ere, before, court.*
Aith, *oath.*
Al, als, *alfo.*
Alhail, alleris, *wholly.*
Allavolie, *at random.*
All yace, allyace, *allies?*
Allyns, *in all ways?*
Alkin, *all kinds of.*
Almofeir, *almoner.*
Almous, *alms.*
Alfwyth, *inftantly.*
Ameis, *leal.*
Amene, *fweet.*
Amorat, *enamoured.*
An, and, *if.*
Anerdis, *adheres.*
Anew, *enough.*
Anker faidell? III. 46.

Anlace, *a large knife, or dagger.*
Anterus, *adventurous.*
A per fe, *unique.*
Apirfmart, *poignant.*
Appoifit, *compofed.*
Areffis, *arrace, tapeftry.*
Art, *point of compafs.*
Artailye, *artillery.*
Affe, *afhes.*
Affiltrie, *axel-tree.*
Affolye, *refolve, abfolve.*
Affucurat, *affured.*
Aftalit, *enftalled.*
At, *that.*
Attour, *moreover, above.*
Avant, *forward,* Fr.
Aucht, *poffeffion.*
Auchtis, *ought.*
Auchtfum, *fome eight, about eight.*
Avenand, *affable.*
Avenantis, *affable men.*
Auld, *old.*
Aunter, *adventure.*
Awaill, I. 58, *return.*
Awevin? II. 5, *error of copy?*
Awmons? III. 155.
Ayldolly? II. 189.
Ay on, *continually.*

R   B. Ba-

B

Bachilere, *knight batcheler.*
Bad, *offered.*
Badlyng, *low fcoundrel.*
Badnyftie? I. 59.
Bail, *grief.*
Bairdit, *caparifoned.*
Bairns, *children.*
Baitand, *pafturing.*
Bakkis, *bats.*
Bald, *bold, impudent.*
Bancours? III. 175.
Bandoun, *prifon.*
Bane, *bearty.*
Banrent, *bunneret.*
Barrace, *trouble.*
Barrat, *forrow.*
Bartanye, *Bretague.*
Bafnet, *helmet.*
Bawburd, *wbore.*
Bazed, *confounded.*
Bedene, *immediately.*
Beevit? III. 79.
Beft, *beaten.*
Begaryit, *ftriped, laced.*
Beheft, *promife.*
Beidmen, *devotees.*
Beild, *fecurity, habitation.*
Beine, *hearty.*
Beir, *barley.*
Beiris? II. 24.—83. *boafts, noife.*
Beit, *help, ftirred.*
Bek, *ftart.*
Beld? III. 165.
Belenes, *fteps afide.*
Belive, *prefently.*
Bellical, *warlike.*
Bemyt, *proclaimed.*
Bene, *good-bumoured.*
Penifoun, *bleffing.*
Bent, *plain, field.*
Berber, *barberry.*
Bere, *outcry.*
Bergane, *battle.*

Berhedis, *bears beads.*
Berle? III. 164.
Bern's, *youtbs.*
Beryel, *beril.*
Befandis, *byzants.*
Befeme, *it feems.*
Befene, *adorned.*
Befs, *bafs.*
Befum, *deformed creature.*
Betaucht, *committed, entrufted.*
Bethleris? III. 174.
Beuch, *bough.*
Beveren? III. 212.
Bewis, *boughs.*
Bewfckeris, *dreffers, adorners.*
Biggit, *builded.*
Bigly, *large.*
Bike, *building.*
Bikker, *fkirmifh.*
Bilt, *belt.*
Binks, *benches.*
Birdis, *damfels.*
Birk, *birch.*
Birnift, *burnifhed.*
Birny, *habergeon.*
Bifmair, *bawd.*
Bittil, *beetle.*
Bla, *deep blue.*
Bladderand, *ftammering.*
Blait, *afbamed.*
Blaitie-bum, *ftupid fellow.*
Blan? III. 118.
Blanchart, *wbite.*
Blanfchit, *bleached.*
Blaucht, *wan.*
Blaving? III. 88.
Blaw, *blown.*
Ble, *bue, complexion.*
Bleirit, *dazzled.*
Blenk, *glance.*
Blent, *glanced.*
Blin, *delay.*
Blithit, *rejoiced.*
Blonk or blouk, *fteed.*
Bloukis, *fteeds.*

Blunket?

Blunket? III. 212.
Blyndit, *blended.*
Blyvar, *believer.*
Blyweft, *blytbeft, moft merry.*
Bob, *bunch.*
Bodword, *tidings.*
Boggil, *fcare crow.*
Boir, *bole.*
Bokeik, *bopeep.*
Bokit, *vomited.*
Boldyn, *fwollen.*
Bolt, *bound, vault.*
Bombard, *cannon.*
Bonde, *flave.*
Bon geur, *good day,* Fr.
Bony, *pretty.*
Borgoyne, *Burgundy?* III. 199.
Bot, *without.*
Boulk, *body,* met. *borfe.*
Bounand, *ready to go.*
Bour, *chamber.*
Fourd, *mock, jeft.*
Boure, *fee* bourd.
Bowis, *folds for cattle.*
Bowfom, *buxom, yielding, affable.*
Bowtit, *bolted.*
Boytour, *bittern?*
Braid, *affault.*
Brais, *embrace.*
Bran, *brawn.*
Brand, *fword.*
Branewod, *mad-brained.*
Brank, *ftrut.*
Brathens? III. 108.
Brayis, *declivities.*
Brechams, *ornaments of neck.*
Breis, *eye-brows.*
Bretynit, *breaking.*
Brewit, *abbreviated,*   .
Breddit? I. 129.
Briffit, *bruifed.*
Brith? III. 73.
Briture? III. 178.
Broch, *fpit.*
Brochis, *kind of buckles.*

Brok, *badger.*
Broudyn? III. 148.
Browftar, *brewer.*
Bruik, *enjoy.*
Brukil, *brittle.*
Brufit, *embroidered.*
Brute, *report.*
Bryhour, *rafcal.*
Brym, *fierce.*
Bubbis, *blaft.*
Bud, *bribe.*
Buit, *help, fupply.*
Buithis, *fhops.*
Bullerand, *weltering.*
Bulling, *boiling.*
Bummil baty, *ftupid drone.*
Bundin, *bound.*
Bunwede? III. 179.
Bur, *bore.*
Bural, *ruftic, boorifh.*
Burde, *table, lady, bride.*
Burdouns, *large ftaves, fpears.*
Burely, *ftout.*
Burgion, *bud.*
Bufkis, *bufhes.*
Bufkit, *made ready.*
But, *without, aim, object.*
Bwillis, *bouls.*
By, *bye, without, befide.*
Bycht? III. 182.
Byhe, *hive.*
Byker, *fkirmifh.*
Bypticit, (biceps) *two headed.*
Byre, *cow houfe.*
Byfning, *ugly.*

C

Cachis, *toffes.*
Caif, *chaff,*
Caiges, *wantons.*
Cale, *broth, caleworts.*
Cairle, *rogue*
Cairt, *car, chariot.*

R 2

Cais,

Cais, *eafe, caufe.*
Campioun, *champion.*
Cankert, *crabbed; peevifb.*
Cant, *merry.*
Canteleinis, *tricks.*
Cappit, *ftupid.*
Caralyngis? III. 180.
Carcat, *necklace.*
Carling, *rogue.*
Carps, *talks, fnatches.*
Carts, *cards.*
Carvel, *floop.*
Caryis, *rides.*
Caffin, *caft, fallen.*
Caftis, *figures.*
Catouris, *providers.*
Cavel, *fcoundrel.*
Celfitude, *highnefs.*
Chaffery, *goods, merchandize.*
Chaftis, *jaws.*
Chapit, *efcaped.*
Chapman, *dealer.*
Charrit, *turned, fent back.*
Cheinyies, *chains.*
Cheis, *chufe.*
Chenit *read* chevit, *achieved.*
Cheffoun, *oppofition?* encheffoun
  is caufe, reafon.
Cheveron? III. 213 *.
Chole? III. 203.
Chop, *fhop.*
Chyppynutie? I. 80.
Chyre, *chair.*
Cite, *city, incite.*
Civile, *Seville.*
Clais, *cloths.*
Clargie, *learning.*
Clatterars, *tale bearers.*

Clatterit, *rattled.*
Claught, *fnatched.*
Cleipit, *called.*
Cleyng? III. 202.
Clippis, *grappling irons.*
Clois, *inclofure, fquare.*
Clowis, *nails, fmall pieces, dales.*
Clowre, *blow, bruife.*
Cod, *pillow.*
Coft, *bought.*
Combure, *inflame.*
Comparges? III. 156.
Conding, *worthy.*
Conftry, *confiftory.*
Copburde, *cupboard of plate.*
Convoy, *trick.*
Copper, *cooper.*
Corbels, *ftone brackets, fupports.*
Corby, *crow.*
Cordenours, *fhoemakers.*
Cors, *body.*
Cors-prefent, *prefent to the church
  on a funeral.*
Coft, *fide.*
Cotter, *cottager.*
Couchit, *inlaid.*
Coverit, *recovered.*
Count, *pretend.*
Courche, couvrechef, *covering for
  the head.*
Couth, *gentle.*
Cow, I. 21, *wifp, bundle.*
Cowclink, *harlot.*
Cowp, *overturn.*
Coy, *ftill, filent.*
Craig, *rock, neck.*
Crak, *chat.*
Cramery, *fluff.*

* From this paffage it appears to have been the ornament or defence of the head of a war-horfe, in the midft of which was an
anlace, or fharp piece of fteel, as is obfervable in miniatures and
other monuments of the times. The heraldic writers miftake the
meaning of cheveron. Is the word from *chef,* (old Fr.) as defending
the head of the horfe?

Crank,

Crank, *roar.*
Creil, *hamper, basket.*
Creische, *sauce.*
Crinis, *shrinks.*
Crochit, *covered.*
Crop, *top.*
Croun, *top of head.*
Crous, *pert.*
Cruikit, *crooked.*
Cuhiculars, *gentlemen of the bed-chamber.*
Cuitchours? II. 163, corr.
Cuities, *ancles.*
Culroun, *silly.*
Culum? II. 69.
Cumen, *come.*
Cummer, *trouble, gossip.*
Cumpanary, *companionship.*
Cumpas, *design.*
Cunning, *covenant.*
Cunyie, *coin.*
Cure, *care, burden.*
Curers. *covers, dishes.*
Curras, *cuirass.*
Curtil, *sluttish.*
Cute, *hoof.*

D

Da, *doe.*
Damais, *Damascus-silk.*
Daffing, *foolery.*
Daf, *foolish.*
Dant? I. 43.
Daw, *day, dawn.*
Debaitit, *fought.*
Defolit, *defiled, dishonoured.*
Degest, *mature.*
Deid, *death.*
Deir, *hurt, door, daring.*
Deis, *raised place of honour in a hall.*
Delf, I. 37, *grave?*
Dellatioun, *delay.*
Delyverlie, *cleverly.*

Dempster, *an officer who pronounces the judgement of a court.*
Dent, *engraven.*
Depair, *impair.*
Deplome, *unfeather.*
Deprysit, *disprised.*
Depured, *pure?*
Derflie, *vigorously.*
Deris, *injures, hurts.*
Derne, *secret.*
Derth, *scarcity.*
Defervis, *serves.*
Destrenyiet, *distracted.*
Det, *duty.*
Devailis, *goes down.*
Devoir, *duty,* Fr.
Dguhare? II. 170, (corrupt.)
Dicht, *drest, adorned.*
Digest, *mature, furnished.*
Dight, *covered.*
Ding, *drive, knock.*
Disjone, *breakfast,* Fr.
Dochly, *duly.*
Docht, *can do.*
Doft, daft, *wanton, foolish.*
Dolent, *sorry.*
Dome, *judge, judgement.*
Dornik, *damasked?*
Dortour, *dormitory.*
Douch spere, Douze Per, *one of the 12 peers.*
Douchtines, *strength, valour.*
Dour, *obstinate, hard.*
Dout, *fear.*
Dow, *can, dove.*
Dowit, *coupled.*
Doytand, *doting.*
Drable? III 172.
Dreifland, *drivelling.*
Dreigh, *slow.*
Diese. *drees, suffers.*
Dreffit, *addressed.*
Drew, *drop.*
Drightin? IIL 114, 118.
Dring, *drive.*

Drint;

Drint, *drowned.*
Drotes? III. 205.
Drowkit, *drenched.*
Drowre, *love-token.*
Dub, *pool.*
Duddroun, *ragged flut.*
Duergh, *dwarf.*
Dulce, *sweet.*
Dulcorait, *sweet.*
Dule, *sorrow.*
Dung, *beaten.*
Dunts, *heavy blows.*
Durandly, *obstinately.*
Durken, *affright.*
Dufchit, *dashed.*
Dyk, *ditch, wall.*
Dynnyt, *made a din.*
Dyntis, *blows.*
Dyocie, *diocese.*
Dyfmel? I. 17.
Dyte, *indite.*
Dyvour, *debtor.*

E

E, *eye.*
Eaty? II. 33.
Ebur, *ivory.* Lat.
Ecleipt *called.*
Efreft? III. 175.
Eighen, *eyes.*
Eild, *old age.*
Eirar, *eafier?*
Eird, *earth.*
Eith, *eafy.*
Elrich, *uncouth, ftrange.*
Enbroued, *embroidered.*
Endored, *heaped.*
Englond-foreft, *Inglewood.*
Enfenye, *cry of war.*
Entailyeit, I. 73, *cut out, formed.*
Erne, *ofprey.*
Ertand? III. 85.
Ery, *fearful.*

Efchewit, *efcaped.*
Efperance, *hope.* Fr.
Eftait, *chair of ftate.*
Efter, *oyfter.*
Ettil, *hint, fhew.*
Evil-payit, *ill-difpofed.*
Evir, *ivory,* I. 71, &c.

F

Fa, *foe.*
Facht? III. 184.
Facund, *eloquent.*
Failen, *want.*
Failyes, *faults, failings.*
Fainy? III. 169.
Fair, effeir, *gefture.*
Fairheid, *fairnefs, beauty.*
Fald, *bow, embrace.*
Fallon, *violent.*
Fallow, *be companion.*
Famyt, *foamed.*
Fane, *fond, mirth.*
Fanis, *vanes.*
Fang, *catch.*
Fanton, *fainting, weaknefs.*
Farar, *fairer.*
Farce, *ftuff.*
Fardils, *pieces.*
Farrand, *becoming.*
Fary, *flutter.*
Fas, *facing.*
Fafle? III. 134.
Faw, *redifh.*
Fax, *locks,* Ifl.
Faynd, *act, do.*
Feckles, *weak.*
Feid, *enmity.*
Feil, *many, fenfe, knowledge.*
Feinyeit, *feigned.*
Feir, *companion, array.*
Feird, *fourth.*
Feirie, *bold.*
Feiris, *affairs, actions.*

Fell,

Fell, *many.*
Fellis, *plains.*
Felloun, *fierce.*
Fend, *fare.*
Fenyie, *feigning, faint.*
Ferlie, *wond r.*
Ferriar. *ferry-man.*
Feſt, *faſten, fx.*
Fey, *unhappy.*
Few, *leaſebold.*
Fidder, *heap, parcel.*
Firth, *field, lawn.*
Flamit, *baniſhed.*
Flatlings, *flatly.*
Flaucht? I. 24.
Fleich, *careſs.*
Fleit, *float, affraid.*
Flekerit, *ſpotted.*
Flemit, *baniſhed.*
Flend, *flee?*
Flet? III. 180.
Flowris, *flower of youth.*
Fludder, *frolic.*
Flynd, III. 69. *flint?*
Flyrand, *fleering, flaunting.*
Flyte, *diſpute, ſcold.*
Fold, *field.*
Fond, *ſilly.*
Fordeiſit, *deafened.*
Fordinnit, *made great din, or noiſe.*
Forfair, *be loſt.*
Forfalt. *loſt, exhauſted.*
Forſneſt, *firſt.*
Fornent, *oppoſite.*
Forout, forouttin, *without.*
Forrow, *before.*
Fors. *ſtrong.*
Forſlitten? III. 38.
Forthink, *repent.*
Forthy, *therefore.*
Foruay, *wander.*
Fouſy, *ditch, Fr.*

Fouth, *plenty.*
Foutour, *raſcal.*
Fow? I. 13. perhaps *club.*
Fow, *full.*
Fra, ſometimes *after.*
Frain, *enquire.*
Fraiſt, *try, ſtrive.*
Fratit, *wrought.*
Fraucht, *cargo.*
Fre, *lady.*
Freinyie, *fringe.*
Fret, *decked.*
Freuch, *petulant?*
Frewp? III. 154.
Frick, *man.*
Fritte? III. 177.
Friwol, *trifling.*
Frody, *cunning.*
Fruſched, *hurtled.*
Frydde, v. *frith.*
Fryme? III. 163. ſeems *ryme, prophecy.*
Fuilyit, *defiled, ſcattered.*
Fuir, *fared.*
Fume, *reliſh.*
Fundun, *marching.*
Fur, *furrow.*
Fute band, *foot guards* *.
Fute pack, *a pack which can be carried by a man on foot.*
Fyellis? I. 112.
Fyke, *vex.*
Fyle, *fowl.*
Fynkle, *periwinkle?* III. 127.
Fyveſum, *ſome five, about five.*

G

Gainand, *fit.*
Gaineſt, ganeſt, *moſt fit.*
Gair, *border.*

* The guard of James V. is, in cotemporary letters,. (Cotton Lib. Cal. B. VI. VII.) called the Fute-band.

Gaiſt,

Gaift, *ghoft.*
Gait, *way.*
Galyeoun, *galley, galeon.*
Gamefons, *armour for legs.*
Gammis, *gums.*
Ganar, *gander.*
Gane, *mouth.*
Ganenyng, *neceffaries, proper articles.*
Ganeftand, *withftand.*
Gant, *gape, yawn.*
Ganyies, *darts.*
Garmoun, *garment.*
Garritour, *watch-man.*
Garfon, *attendant.*
Gart, *caufed.*
Garth, *garden.*
Gauckit, *ftupid.*
Gawmond, *jig, quick dance.*
Gay, *go, gay lady.*
Gearking, *vain.*
Geck, *mock.*
Geil, *jelly.*
Geir, *armour, cloathing.*
Gent, *gentle, elegant.*
Gide, *attire.*
Gillie, *boy ?*
Gin, *ingenuity.*
Gird, *ftrike.*
Glaid, *went fwiftly, glided.*
Glaiks, *wandering light reflected from a mirror, &c.*
Glavis, *fwords.*
Glede, *flame.*
Gleit, *fhine.*
Glew, *glee.*
Glois ? III. 12.
Gloppe, *fot ?*
Glowris, *ftares.*
Gnappit, *chirped.*
Godbairn, *godchild.*
Goift, *fpirit.*
Gome, *warrior, man.*
Gorbets, *young birds.*

Gormand, *gluttonous.*
Goffe, *goffip.*
Gouand, *gazing.*
Goums, *gums.*
Gouwan, *daify.*
Gowk, *cuckow.*
Gowl, *growl.*
Gowp, *mouthful.*
Grat, *weeped.*
Graggit ? II. 251.
Grainter ? II. 223.
Graith, *drefs, armour.*
Gram, *trouble, tumult.*
Grameft, *moft warlike.* III.
Granate, *cloth of a fine dye.* I. 63.
Gratnis ? III. 164.
Grede, *cry.*
Grein, *defire.*
Greit, *weep.*
Grendes, *grandees ?*
Greues, *groves.*
Grew, *Greek.*
Grie, *degree, ftep.*
Grip, *poffeffion.*
Grow, *fhudder.*
Grulingis, *grovelling.*
Grumis, *men.*
Gruntill ? II. 69.
Grunyie, *nofe.*
Grvis ? I. 84.
Grylles, *cuts.*
Gryfs, *pig.*
Gucke, *play the fool.*
Guckit and gend, *foolifh and wild.*
Guddame, *grand-mother.*
Gude havings, *good behaviour.*
Gudget ? III. 33.
Gmllings ? II. 193.
Guerdon, *reward, guarantee.*
Gukkit, *ftupid.*
Gut, *goat.*
Gyde, *guiding, management.*
Gyrcarling ? II. 18. *fome ideal being.*

H. Hadder,

H

Hadder, *heath.*
Hafles, *without poffeffions?*
Hag, *knotch.*
Hailfome, *wholefome.*
Haims, *collars.*
Hain, *fave.*
Haire, *high.* Ill.
Hait, *beat.*
Hale, *whole, entire.*
Halflings, *half.*
Halking, *hawking.*
Halfis, *throats.*
Hap, *chance.*
Harborit, *lodged.*
Harlots, *fcoundrels.*
Harlry? III. 174.
Harnes, *harnefs, armour.*
Harnis, *brains.*
Harn-pan, *head, fcull.*
Hat, *hit.*
Hate, *hot.*
Hathil? III. 104. 107. 202. 225.
Hatterit, *fhattered.*
Haw, *dark-blue.*
Hawtane, *haughty.* Fr.
He, *high.*
Hecht, *called, promife.*
Heich, *high.*
Heichtit, *raifed.*
Heidgeir, *head-attire.*
Heilded, *held, raifed.*
Heily, *filly.*
Heir, *here, bear: lord, mafter.*
Hen-wife, *woman who takes care of hens.*
Henfeman, *henchman, clofe attendant.*
Herbier, *herbory, garden, arbour.*
Here, *ravage, ruin.*
Here-geild, *right of lord of manor on a new fucceffion.*
Herlie, *heartily.*
Herts, *harts.*
VOL. III.

Heryis, *ravage, wafte.*
Hefs, *hoarfe.*
Heft, *command.*
Hether, *hence.*
Hething, *mockery.*
Heuir, *whore.*
Hewch, *hewed.*
Hewis? III. 45. *fhapes, fhades?*
Hewit, *hevit, raifed.*
Heynd, *elegant.*
Highen, *by.*
Hiddil, *hiding, concealment.*
Hint, *caught.*
Ho! *ftop! ftie.*
Hobby? III. 175.
Hochis, *heels, boughs.*
Holked, *Followed.*
Holtis, *bights.*
Holyng, *holly.*
Hom, *them.*
Hone, *delay.*
Honir, *f.* hovir, *hover.*
Hote, *promife.*
Hovand, *hovering.*
Houlat, *owl.*
How, *deep, bunch, hood.*
Howis, *boughs.*
Hoyyes, Oyez, Fr. *proclamation.*
Hurde, *hoard, heap.*
Hurftis, *woods.*
Hurthy? III. 184.
Hufbands, *yeomen.* villani, *bound to a houfe or farm.*
Hufe? III. 159.
Huttock? III. 61.
Huwes, *holts, hills.*
Hy, *bafte,*
Hyne, *hence.*
Hynefurth, *henceforth.*
Hyrald, *fee* Heregeild.

I J

Ja, *jay.*
S

Jack,

Jack, *iron doublet.*
Jaip, *trick, mockery.*
Jangle and jak, *at random.*
Jangler, *railer.*
Japane, *playing tricks.*
Ilk, *each.*
Ilkane, *each one.*
Impesche, *binder.*
In, *dwelling.*
Incendit, *kindled.*
Infeane? II. 16.
Ingent, *large.* Lat.
Ingrave, part. *cut out.*
Innis, *house, habitation.*
Inore? III. 213.
Intane, *taken in.*
Interlocuture, *sentence.*
Inteft, *untold?*
Invaird, *put in ward, prison.*
In vairt, *inwards.*
Inwith, *within.*
Joe, *sweet-heart.*
Jonet, *jennet, Spanish horse.*
Jowkit, *joked.*
Irke, *vext.*
Ithandly, *vigorously.*
Juglour, *juggler, magician.*
Junctures, *joints, seams.*
Jupert, *jeopardy.*
Juxters, *jokers.*

K

Kellis, *cawl, woman's head-dress.*
Kellit, *called?*
Ken, *know.*
Kenettes, *bounds.*
Kewis, kowis, *usages, practice.*
Kid, kythed, *shewn.*
Kilt, *tuck.*
Kinrikis, *kingdoms.*
Kirtil, *close-gown.*
Kist, *chest.*
Kittoks, *dalliers.*

Knaspkaw, *knapsack.*
Knoppit, *with knobs.*
Koddis, *cushions, pillows.*
Kow, *fee* Kewis.
Kowschot, *ring-dove.*
Ky, *cows.*
Kynd, *nature.*
Kyrnellis, *battlements.*
Kyth, *shew : people.*

L

Lachter, *letcher.*
Ladroun, *lazy knave.*
Ladry, *idle lads.*
Laif, *rest.*
Laige, *liege subject.*
Laik? I. 77.
Lair, *teaching.*
Lairbair, *dirty fellow.*
Lait, laik, *want.*
Laithles, *unmannerly.*
Lak, *want, defect.*
Lakkest, *meanest.*
Lakkis, *undervalues.*
Lame, *lamb.*
Lamenry, *wanton love.*
Landwart, *rustic.*
Lane? I. 41.—*leave.*
Lansit, *darted.*
Lard, *lord,* feigneur.
Lardun, *lardor.*
Lat, *slop.*
Lathest, *most lothsome.*
Latious, *wide, free.*
Laver to layre? III. 225. *eaft to*
  weft?
Laud, *praise.*
Lap, *leaped.*
Laucht, *taken.*
Laus, *(lows,) fires?*
Lawe, *below.*
Lawit, *laymen.*
Layke, *paint.*

Layne,

Layne, *ly.*
Laytes, *geſtures, behaviour.*
Ledder, *leather.*
Leich, *phyſician.*
Leid, *learning, eloquence, perſon, region.*
Leif, *live, believe.*
Leil, *true, truſty.*
Leind? I. 41.
Leir, *learn.*
Leirit, *learned.*
Leiſe me, *my bleſſing on.*
Leit, *did let, did ſet.*
Lemand, *ſhining.*
Lemman, *lover.*
Lent, *dwell, be.*
Leſing, *lying.*
Left, *leaſt.*
Let, *hindrance.*
Levar, *rather, fleſh.* See Lyre.
Leud, *unlearned.*
Levin, *living.*
Leving, *idle boaſts.*
Leynd, *dwell.*
Libberly? I. 11.
Licame, *body.*
Licence, *leave.*
Licht, *light-headed.*
Lidder, *ſlow, lazy.*
Lie, *lee, calm.*
Lig, *ly.*
Liggis, *leagues,* I. 64.
Likand, *pleaſant.*
Limmer, *ſcoundrel.*
Lippen, *truſt, depend.*
Lis, *leſſen.*
Lite, *little.*
Loſe, *praiſe,* III.
Logh, *low.*
Loif, *honour, praiſe.*
Loiffit, *loofed.*
Lokin, *locked up?*
Lony, *(loun,) low.*
Lopd, *leaped.*
Lore, *learning, ſkill; low.*

Lorer, *laurel.*
Lorimer, *ſaddler.*
Loſe, *praiſe.*
Loun, *rogue.*
Loup, *leap.*
Low, *love, flame.*
Lowabill, *laudable.*
Lowpit, *wreathed.*
Lowre, *ſtoop.*
Lowry, *fox.*
Lowtit, *bowed.*
Lufe, *palm.*
Luferay, *livery.*
Lugs, *ears.*
Lumis, *looms.*
Lunyie, *loins.*
Lurdan, *impudent knave.*
Luſt, *deſire.*
Luſtelie, *comelyly.*
Luſtie, *comely, handſome, deſireable.*
Ly, *life.*
Lyamis, *reins.*
Lychtlyand, *holding lightly.*
Lyking, *pleaſure.*
Lymnaris, *poles of a chariot.*
Lympet, III. 187.
Lynd, *boughs, lime-tree.*
Lyng, *line, ſtrait courſe.*
Lyre, *fleſh.*
Lyte, *little.*
Lyth, *liſten.*
Lytil wie, *ſhort time.*

M

Machit, *matched.*
Macrell, *bawd.*
Maggies, *jades.*
Magry, *in ſpite,* Fr.
Mahoms, *Mahomets.*
Maiglit, *mangled.*
Maik, *match, companion.*
Mail, *rent.*
Mair, *more.*

S 2

Mairattour,

Mairattour, *moreover.*
Mais, *makes.*
Mait, *confounded.*
Mal-eis, *diforder.*
Maling, *are malignant.*
Manance, *menace.*
Mandrit, *tame.*
Mane, *ftrength, moan.*
Mangit, *maimed, ftupid, rimes to hangit.*
Mankit, *wanted,* Fr.
Map-mond, *world,* met.
Marres, *morafs.*
Marrow, *match.*
Martis, *Mars's.*
Marvill, *marble.*
Mavefie, *Malmfey.*
Mavis, *thrufh.*
Mawments, *idols.*
May, *maid.*
Megir? I. 71.
Meine, *hint, lament.*
Mekil, *large, many.*
Mel, *fpeak,* (mail, *concilium.)*
Membronis? III. 174.
Menfe, *decency, worth, adorn.*
Mensful, *decent.*
Menfkit, *arranged.*
Merkit, *marched, marked.*
Merle, *black-bird.*
Mes, *mafs.*
Midlit, *mingled.*
Mint, *try.*
Mirk, *dark.*
Misfarne, *mifmanaged.*
Miffettand, *unbecoming.*
Miffive, *letter fent.*
Mifter, *need.*
Mobil, *moveables.*
Moch? I. 60.
Mokrand? I. 13.
Mold, *earth.*
Mon, *muft.*
Monie, *many.*
Montur, *fteed,* Fr.

Mort, *dead,* Fr.
Mot, *might.*
Mouar, *mocker.*
Moutit? I. 60.
Mow, *mouth.*
Mowis, *mocks.*
Moyen, *means,* Fr.
Muillis, *woman's flippers.*
Mum, *hint.*
Mundane, *worldly.*
Mundie? III. 37.
Munyeoun, *minion.*
Murle, *moulder.*
Murmel, *murmur.*
Mufkane? I. 60. 66. 79.
Muftages, *muftachios.*
Mute? I. 46.
Myith, *mix.*
Myn, *lefs,* Lat.
Mynny, *mamma.*
Mynt, *offer.*
Myffel, III. 14, *veil, or mafque?*

N

Navell, *blow.*
Naxte, *nafty.*
Neb, *beak.*
Nebbis, *beaks.*
Neiris, *kidneys.*
Nemmyt, *named.*
Neruit, *inwrought?*
Nevin, *name, repeat.*
Nold, *would not.*
Nolt, *horned cattle.*
Nor I, *may I perifh if I would not.*
Not, I. 55, *knew not.*
Novellis, *news.*
Noy, *Noah.*
Nycht, *approach.*
Nychtit, *night fell.*
Nyte, *deny.*
Nytherit, *turned down?*

O Obleffing,

O

Oblessing, *obligation.*
Oist, *host, assembly, landlord.*
Olk, *week.*
One, wone, I. 71, *wane, car.*
On hede. *unheededly.*
Ontray, *betray.*
Oonly, *alone.*
Ordinance, *array.*
Orere, ourere, *arrear, fall back.*
Orphany (orfevre), *gold work?*
Osillis? III. 177.
Ostend, *shew,* Lat.
Overhy, *purchase pardon.*
Ouirset, *covered.*
Ouirsyle, *beguile.*
Ouirthort, *athwart.*
Ourcorss, *across.*
Out-braid. *burst out.*
Owder, *either.*
Owis, *belongs.*
Oy, *grand-daughter.*

P

Faddois, *frogs.*
Paik, *strike.*
Pair, *impair.*
Pa sand, *heavy? Fr.*
Paist, *repast.*
Palyeoun, *pavilion.*
Pance, *think, besitate.*
Pantit, *painted.*
Pantouns, *slippers.*
Pape, papingo, *parroquet.*
Pappis, *breasts.*
Parage, *lineage.*
Pardonar, *seller of pardons.*
Parlour, *conversation, debate.*
Parsillit, *striped.*
Pase, *pass.*
Pattrel, *breast leather.*
Paven, *pavine, measure of a dance.*

Payit, *disposed.*
Pedder, *pedlar.*
Peggral, *petty.*
Peild, *ball.*
Pellokis, *bullets.*
Pelour, *thief.*
Persseil, *penon.*
Peranter, *peradventure, perchance.*
Perles, *peerless.*
Perqueir, *par cœur, off hand.*
Perre? III. 213.
Pess, *Easter,* Fr.
Pewtene, *whore.*
Picht, *pitched.*
Piis (Flanders), *pease, beans.*
Pill, *pillage.*
Plage, *quarter, paint.*
Plait, *mail.*
Plane, *full,* Fr.
Plant, *planted, decked.*
Plate. *knock.*
Flayseir, *playfellow.*
Pleid, *controversy.*
Plent, *complaint.*
Plenyie, *complain.*
Plevaris, *plovers.*
Plicht, *pledge.*
Plie, *plead.*
Poid, *poet?*
Polite, *polished.*
Ponnyis? III. 187.
Port, *gate.*
Porteris, *portouns, mass-book.*
Portrait, *painted.*
Portraiture, *lineaments.*
Poveral, *mob*
Pourit, *impoverished.*
Powand, *pulling*
Powderit. *sprinkled.*
Powin? III. 172.
Practik, *art.*
Prais, *press, tumult.*
Prece'us, *excells*
Preclair, *celebrated.*
Preif, *prove.*

Prene,

Prene, *pin.*
Prete, *ready,* Fr.
Prieſt, *preſſed.*
Pris, *value.*
Prow, *proweſs, worth.*
Pryme, *morning.*
Puddlit, *ſpattered.*
Puird, *impoveriſhed.*
Pulchritude, *beauty.*
Pundare, poynder, *ſeizer in diſtreſs.*
Punic, *Phœnician dye, fine purple.*
Pure, *poor.*
Pyats, *magpies.*
Pylefat, *brewing vat.*

Q

Quaid ? I. 81.
Quaif, *quoif, cover.*
Quaint, *curious, acute.*
Quells, *yells.*
Quemit, *fitted cloſe.*
Quhert ? III. 92. 193.
Queſts, *noiſe of hounds.*
Quhare, *place.*
Quhil, *untill.*
Quuik, *quaked.*

R

Rachis, *hounds.*
Radder, *more red.*
Raddour, *timidity :* rubor, pudor.
Radious, *radiant.*
Raid, *road.*
Raif, *riven.*
Raikit, *roved.*
Rair, *roar.*
Raithly, *ſoon.*
Rak, *fault.*
Rammal, *ſhrubs, bramble ?*
Ramyt, *ſkouted.*
Randonit, *arranged.*

Rane, *noiſe.*
Rangald, *crowd, mob.*
Raris, *roars.*
Raſſit, *razed.*
Rax, *ſtretch.*
Raylit, *bordered.*
Rayne-bow, *rain-bow;* to fit on,
  I. 17; *to be exalted to the utmoſt.*
Rebald, *raſcal.*
Rebawkit, *rebuked.*
Rechas, *hunter's muſic.*
Red, *affraid, parted.*
Redding, *parting.*
Regiment, *rule.*
Reid, *pipe, counſel.*
Reidſet ? III. 196.
Reiſt, *caught.*
Reik, *ſmoke.*
Reim, *realm.*
Reird, *noiſe, tumult.*
Reirdit, *reared.*
Reke, *reach.*
Reknand, *taking care, adviſing
  with.*
Relyie, *rally.*
Remords, *remembers.*
Remyllis, *blows.*
Renk, *perſon.*
Renſe, *Rheniſh.*
Repair, *company.*
Repurcuſt, *repelled.*
Res, *race, courſe.*
Reſpirature, *re-inſpirer.*
Reſſett, *received, refuge.*
Rethnas, *prey ?*
Rever, *robber.*
Rew, *pity.*
Rewſcand, *rouzing.*
Rice, *ruſhes, ſhrubs.*
Rick, *matter.*
Rickittis, *heaps.*
Rike, *rich.*
Ring, *rein, region.*
Rink, *courſe.*
Rink-roome, *place of tourney, courſe*
Riolyſe,

Riolyfe, *feems from royal, princely persons.*
Rippat, *tumult.*
Roch, *rough.*
Rode, *complexion.*
Roife, *fiream ?*
Rok, *diftaff.*
Ron, *rofier ?*
Rone, *run, path.*
Roploch, raploch, *coarfe cloth.*
Round, *whifper.*
Roundel, *a round table.*
Rouftie, *rufty.*
Routit, *roared.*
Rowan, *old jade.*
Rowand, *rolling wantonly.*
Rowmed, *roamed.*
Rowpit, *fcreamed.*
Rowth, *rough.*
Roy, *king,* Fr.
Royk (reek), *fog, fmoke.*
Rubyatour, *robber.*
Rude, *erofs.*
Ruggis, *drags.*
Ruiks, *rooks.*
Rumifching, *rumbling.*
Runt, *trunk of a tree or plant.*
Rufe, *boaft.*
Ryale, *royal, royal perfonage.*
Rybees ? III. 198.
Ryfe, *plenty.*
Ryne ? III. 77.

S

Sacht, *made peace.*
Saghtil, *make peace.*
Saikles, *innocent.*
Saill, *ball,* Fr.
Saip, *foap.*
Sairnes, *forenefs, pain.*

Sale, *affault.*
Sall ? III. 181. *fiall, ftole ?*
Salf, *protect.*
Samekil, *fo much.*
Sane, *fay.*
Sanorous, *favoury.*
Sanrare ? III. 155.
Sark, *fbirt, fbift.*
Saynd, *faying, meffage.*
Sayndis ? III. 82. See Saynd.
Sayne, *fave. blefs.*
Saucht, *fafety, peace.*
Saudel ? III. 213.
Saull prow, *benefit of foul.*
Saw, *faying, fpeech.*
Scarlet, *fine cloth ; white fcarlet occurs in old writers,*
Schalk, *knight* *.
Schankis, *legs.*
Schaw, *grove.*
Scheddit, *fireamed forth.*
Scheidis, *fhields.*
Schene, *fplendid.*
Schenkit, *burft.*
Schent, *troubled.*
Schiere, *cheer.*
Schone, *fhoes.*
Schouris, *forrows.*
Schrowd, *drefs.*
Scrycht, *fhrieked.*
Scule, *fchool.*
Se, *fea.*
Sedis, *proceeds.*
Sege, *man.*
Seif, *feive.*
Seil, *happinefs.*
Seindle, *feldom.*
Seir, *many.*
Seis, I. 54. *feats, places ?*
Selcough, *firange.*
Sele, *feal.*
Sembillit, *affembled.*

* The word, as in *Marifcbalk,* &c. originally meaned *fervant,* as does alfo *knecht,* or knight.

Sen,

Sen, *fenfyne, fince.*
Send, *meffage.*
Senthis, *bence.*
Senyie, *affize.*
Septentrional, *northern,* Lat.
Serk, *fbirt.*
Service, I. 8. *divine fervice, mafs.*
Set, *appoint.*
Sewans, *flummery.*
Sewch, *gulf, ditch.*
Shed, *parted.*
Shore. *fchore, threat.*
Sib, *akin.*
Sickand, *fighing.*
Sickerlie, *furely.*
Sigonale ? III. 182.
Silit ? III. 90.
Siller, *campy.*
Singe, *fign.*
Site, *forrow.*
Skaiplarie, *fcapulary.*
Skance? III. 38.
Skap, *fcalp, fcull.*
Skar, *fcare-crow.*
Skarth, *hermaphrodite, fea-fowl.*
Ske'p, *blow.*
Skirp, *gibe.*
Skoird, *fhaved, cut clofe.*
Skrymmorie? I. 80.
Sknwes, *fhaws, groves.*
Skyre, *fheer, quite.*
Slaid, *vale.*
Slaik, *remit, quench.*
Slatit, *let loofe.*
Slidder, *flippery.*
Slokkin, *quench.*
Slop, *breach, gap.*
Sloppit, *made breaches.*
Slyke? I. 60.
Smaddit, *maddened.*
Smaik, *fneaking fellow.*
Smiddy, *fmithy.*
Smuird, *fmothered.*
Smure, *fmother, be concealed.*
Smy, *paltry fellow.*

Sol, *the fun.* Lat. *foil.*
Soland, *folan-goofe, gannet.*
Soles, *folace.*
Solift, *folicited.*
Solpit, *fobbed.*
Solyeing, *folution.*
Sone, *fun, foon.*
Soner, *truft.*
Sophine, *fophiftry.*
Sowlpit, *fleeped.*
Sowmit, *fwimmed.*
Sowttar, *fhoe-maker.*
Spaiks, *fparks.*
Spail, *fpell, blow.*
Spalis, *fplinters.*
Spare, *barren.*
Speanlie, *wife.*
Specht, *wood-pecker.*
Speir, *fphere, fpear, afk.*
Speirlt, *afked.*
Sperk halkis, *fparrow-hawks.*
Sporne? III. 104.
Sprent, *fplit.*
Springald, *ftripling.*
Spuilyet, *defpoiled.*
Stad, *eftate.*
Stakkerit, *ftaggered.*
Stalwart, *ftout.*
Stanerie, *gravelly.*
Stank, *ditch.*
Stapalis, *faftenings?*
Stark, *ftrong.*
Steadings, *farms.*
Steid, *eftate, place, part.*
Steir, *ftout.*
Sterne, *ftern man*
Sterny, *ftarry.*
Stevin, *voice.*
Stichling, *chirping.*
Sting, *pole, pike.*
Stithil, *fteer?*
Stithly, *ftoutly.*
Stock, *trunk of a tree.*
Stoppit, *refifted.*
Stotit, *ftaggered.*

Stout,

Stoup, *can, pitcher.*
Stour, *tumult, battle.*
Stouth, *stealth.*
Straucht, *stretched.*
Strontly, *strictly.*
Stry, *strive, oppose.*
Strynd, *issue, race.*
Sturt, *trouble.*
Stuval? II. 221.
Styl, *title.*
Stylit, *honoured.*
Stynt, *stop.*
Suage, *assuage, weaken.*
Suave, *sweet.*
Suawe, *so.*
Sucker, *sugar.*
Succquedry, *presumption.*
Sufron, *sufferance.*
Sunyie, *care,* Fr.
Suppryfit, *suppress, borne down.*
Surrey, *Syria.*
Swages, *sway, turn.*
Sware, *neck.*
Swalterit, *sweltered.*
Sweir, *lazy.*
Swefche? I. 212.
Swingeour, *braggadocio, brave.*
Swink, *toil.*
Swire, *neck.*
Swonkand, *swimming.*
Swyth, *instantly.*
Syde, *long.*
Syik, *gutter.*
Sylit, *covered.*
Syll, *threshold.*
Sylour, *silver;* but *see* siller.
Syment, *cement.*
Syne, *since.*
Sypyns, *small drink, weak beer.*
Syre, *lord.*
Syfe, *times.*
Syth, *times.*

T

Tabil, *draughts.*
Table, I. 20. *tablets.*
Taburne, *tabor.*
Taftais, *taffety.*
Taggit, *pulled.*
Taiklit, *furnished with tackle.*
Tain, *taken.*
Tairfull, *sorrowful.*
Taking, *token.*
Tarlochs? III. 47.
Tartain, *tertian.*
Tasses, *cups.*
Tathis? III. 105.
Teims, *empties.*
Teind, *tyth.*
Teir, *fatigue.*
Teirful, *fatiguing.*
Temyt, *left empty.*
Tene, *sorrow.*
Tent, *heed.*
Tent-taill, I. 75, *tenth deal, tenth part?*
Teuch, *tough.*
The, I. 4, *thrive.*
Thede, *business?*
The kit, *thatched, covered.*
Thewit, *disposed.*
Thift lowis? I. 141.
Thill, III. 187.
Thir, *these.*
Thirlage, *bondage.*
Tho, I. 58, &c. *then,* I. 94, *these.*
Thocht, *though.*
Tholit, *suffered.*
Thra, *cross.*
Thraw? I. 71.—I. 297. *pang.*
Thrawin, *misshaped, awry.*
Thril, *thral,-servant,* ISl.
Thrift, *thrust, prest.*
Thyne, *thence.*
Ticht, *tied.*
Tight, *fixt, tie :*

T Tint,

Tint, *lost.*
Tirlit, *twisted.*
Titgandis? III. 152.
Tocher, *portion.*
Tod, *fox.*
Tone, *taken.*
Torfeir? III. 104.
Traist, *trust.*
Trane, *stratagem.*
Tranoynt, *pass.*
Trawyntit, *passed.*
Trencheour, *head of a spear,* Fr.
Trestle, *support.*
Trentals, *thirty masses.*
Trewker? II. 53. correct.
Triste, *appointed place.*
Tristres, v. Triste.
Trow, *believe.*
Trumpours, *deceivers.*
Tuglit. *fatigued.*
Tuich, *tough, averse.*
Tuigh, *touch.*
Turs, *bundle up.*
Tufches, *bands.*
Twane, tway, *two.*
Twistis, *twigs.*
Twitching, *touching.*
Twyn, *part.*
Tyde, *time.*
Tydiar, *cleaner.*
Tyime, (timbre) *crest?*
Tyld, *cover.*
Tyldit, *covered.*
Tyne, *lose.*
Tyfe, *entice.*
Tyte, *quick.*
Tythandis, *tidings.*

U V

Vacains, *vacation.*
Vagers, *soldiers.*
Vaikis, *wait.*
Vail, *bow.*

Varlots, *valets.*
Vassalage, *followers, honour.*
Ventaill, *visor.*
Ver, *spring, worse.*
Verement, *verity, truth.*
Veres, *glasses?*
Vergers, *orchards,* Fr.
Vernage? III. 216.
Vesie, *see.*
Vetit, *forbidden,* Lat.
Veug, (vogy) *pert.*
Vilipend, *vilify.*
Virgultis, *bushes.*
Umbethocht, *bethought.*
Umest, *upmost, upper.*
Umquhyle, *sometimes.*
Unefe, *hardly.*
Uneth, *uneasily, difficultly.*
Unfane, *unjoyful, sad.*
Unfute fair? I. 3. *the passage seems corrupt.*
Unheilded, *uncovered.*
Unquart? III. 96.
Unfile? II. 127. 202. *unlucky?*
Unfaucht, *not at ease.*
Unfelyable, *unassailable.*
Unwemmit? I. 95.
Vow! *Sure!*
Upaland, *upland, rustic.*
Upbred, *set out.*
Uphald, *support.*
Upheit, *raised.*
Ure, *ore.*
Utterit, I. 165, *reared?*
Vult, *face,* Lat.

W

Wace, *was.*
Wage, *bargain.*
Wailis, *avails.*
Wailit, *chose.*
Waine and quheil, *waggon and wheel,* I. 17, *proverbial.*

Wairdit,

Wairdit, *imprifoned.*
Wait, *wet.*
Waith, *wandering.*
Waits, wotes, *knows.*
Wakar, *walker, cloth-dreffer.*
Wald, *would.*
Wallie, *valley, wavy.*
Wallis, *wawis, waves.*
Wallowit, *withered.*
Walterand, *weltering.*
Waly, *well, good fortune.*
Wamfler, *debauchee.*
Waud, *fcourge.*
Wander ? II. 10. 68. *mifhap ?*
Wandreth, *fee* wander.
Wane, *yearn.*
Wappit, *warped, turned.*
War, *worfe, wary, were.*
Warie, *get worfe, curfe.*
Warlieft, *moft wary.*
Warlo, *magician.*
Warne, *prevent.*
Warwolf, lycanthropus, *a perfon transformed to a wolf.*
Water-cail, *foup-meagre.*
Wayeft, *moft woeful.*
Wayis, *woe is.*
Waymyng ? III. 201.
Wed, *pledge, wager.*
Wee, *fee* wy.
Weilis, *well is, it is well with.*
Weill, *well, a well.*
Weir, *delay, war, were.*
Weird, *fate.*
Weirlie, *warlike.*
Wemeles, *without appetite ?*
Wend, *knew, go.*
Werd, *become, befall.*
Were, *ward, keep.*
Wermis, *fnakes.*
Weiray, *worry.*
Wefch, *wafh.*
Weft, *wift, fuppofed.*
Wetfhod, *with wet fhoes.*
Weuch, *wes.*

Whelen, *who ?*
Wicht, *ftrong.*
Wid, *wager.*
Widdie, *halter.*
Widdyfow, *knavifh.*
Wilfum, *folitary.*
Wirdy, *worthy.*
Wirk, *work.*
Wifh, wufh, *wafhed.*
Wifs, *inform.*
Wittin, *known.*
With thy, *with this, [condition.]*
Wlonkeft, *moft adorned.*
Wlowk, *lady ?*
Wobftar, *weaver.*
Wod, *mad.*
Wodroifs, *a favage ?*
Wol, *wool.*
Womenting, *lamenting.*
Wone, *refidence.*
Worchen, *work.*
Worryours, *warriors.*
Wortheleth, *worthy.*
Worthin, *waxed, become.*
Worthis, *muft.*
Wound, *wondrous, exceeding.*
Wout, (vult) *face, Lat.*
Wox, *became.*
Wraighly, *untowardly.*
Wraik, *avenge.*
Wraith, *wroth.*
Wrappit, *intwined.*
Wregh, *wretched.*
Wreth, *wretch.*
Wrichtis, *carpenters.*
Wrokin, *avenged.*
Wrynkis, *windings, tricks.*
Wfche, *bufh, filence ?*
Wy, *wight, perfon.*
Wyfe, *old woman.*
Wvle, *entice.*
Wylecot, *under petticoat.*
Wynd, *wight, perfon.*
Wynnit, *dwelt.*
Wynfik ? III. 133.

Wyte,

Wyte, *blame.*

Y

Yaid, *gave.*
Yairnis, *yearns for, defires.*
Yane thore? III. 169.
Yauland, *yelling.*
Ybet, *fupplied.*
Ydy, *eddy, pool.*

Yeid, *went.*
Yeild, *a recompence.*
Yemyt, *kept.*
Yet, *gate.*
Yeves, *gives.*
Yimmit, *kept.*
Ying, *young.*
Yomerand, *muttering.*
Yowtheid, *youth-hood, ftate of youth.*

T H E   E N D.

Publifhed by the fame Editor,

Select Scotish Ballads, 2 Vols. 1783.

Ancient Scotish Poems, from the Maitland MS. 2 Vols. 1786.

The Bruce, or the Hiftory of Robert I. King of Scotland; written by John Barbour, Archdeacon of Aberdeen in 1375; the firft genuine Edition, from a MS. dated 1489. 3 Vols. 1790.

www.ingramcontent.com/pod-product-compliance
Lightning Source LLC
Chambersburg PA
CBHW030400270326
41926CB00009B/1189